Business for teenagers

A guide to entrepreneurship and start-ups for teenagers

With a fun and accessible approach

Marcel Aoudi

CONTENTS

Why this book ?....................

The basics of entrepreneurship....................

What is entrepreneurship?......................

What is a start-up?.................................

Advice for future entrepreneurs ....

Company classification....................................

Different types of company...................................

Starting a business................................

Essential entrepreneurial skills............................

Creativity and innovation.....................................

Tips for unleashing creativity and cultivating innovation ....

Time and priority management...................................

Tips for managing your time like a pro ....

Communication and negotiation skills...........................

Tips for honing your communication and negotiation skills .....

Managing income and expenses..........................

Strategies for managing your finances ....

Company management...................................

Employee and partner management ....

Creating a winning team ....

Strategic planning and decision-making............................

 The Art of Strategic Planning ....

Business performance assessment and risk management.......

 Performance evaluation ....

Practical advice on how to succeed as a teenage entrepreneur....

Find mentors and support networks ....

The Importance of Mentors: Guides in the dark...........................

Balancing entrepreneurship with studies and other activities and commitments ....

Avoid common mistakes made by young entrepreneurs.................

 From idea to reality ....

Practical exercises......................................

Some useful resources ....

Conclusion.................................

Why this book?

Entrepreneurship isn't just for adults wearing smart suits in luxurious offices. Teenagers too have fertile ground to develop their ideas, express their creativity and create something meaningful. But why should you, as a teenager, be interested in entrepreneurship? Let's take a look at some of the reasons why.

Entrepreneurship offers a unique opportunity to create something that's just like you, something you've dreamed of. Imagine being able to bring your ideas to life and see the concrete results of your work. Think of your favorite band. They started out somewhere, often in a garage. By becoming an entrepreneur, you create your own "garage" where your dreams come to life.

School is important, but nothing beats work experience. By immersing yourself in the world of entrepreneurship, you'll learn lessons that aren't necessarily taught in textbooks. You'll learn how to make decisions, solve problems and deal with unexpected situations.

Entrepreneurship is like a video game. At each level, you learn something new, but in the real world. This gives you practical skills that will come in handy whatever career you choose. Creativity, time management, and communication, problem-solving: these skills will serve you throughout your life.

 Imagine you're planning a surprise party for a friend. You have to plan, coordinate and keep it a secret. Entrepreneurship is like throwing the best surprise party of your life.

By becoming an entrepreneur, you can inspire other young people to follow their dreams. You become a source of inspiration for those who believe that age is no barrier to success. You can become the hero of your own entrepreneurial story, and inspire other young people to write theirs.

Going into business as a teenager means discovering an entirely new world, full of exciting opportunities and challenges. It's an adventure that lets you grow, learn and become the best version of yourself. So, are you up for the challenge?

Encouraging creativity

Entrepreneurship is much more than a series of numbers and a business plan, it's a canvas on which you can paint your most creative and innovative ideas. Teenagers are naturally gifted with a vivid imagination and an entrepreneurial spirit that enables them to turn their dreams into reality. Imagine you're passionate about video games, but you still feel like there's something you're missing. Entrepreneurship will enable you to create the game you've always wanted to play, with your own rules.

Acquiring business skills gives you creative power. You can take that great idea you had one day and turn it into something concrete. Entrepreneurship provides the tools you need to turn those ideas into reality. Take your favorite band, for example. They don't just imagine songs, they create them. Being an entrepreneur is like being the leader of your own band, whose main theme is creativity.

Many teenagers have a burning passion, whether it's technology, fashion, music or something else. Entrepreneurship paves the way for turning these passions into a successful business. It's the transition from "I love it" to "I've created something I love". If you're passionate about fashion, imagine creating a clothing line that reflects your own style. Entrepreneurship gives you the power to turn your passion into reality.

Entrepreneurship creates an environment where young people's ideas are valued. You're not just a spectator in the business world, but also an important player. That's where your voice counts, even if you're under 18.

Entrepreneurship opens the door to a world where young people's creativity is not just appreciated, but celebrated. It's an exciting journey where every idea, no matter how crazy, has the potential to become the next big thing. So get ready to unleash your creative talent and transform the world with your unique ideas.

Building self-confidence

Entrepreneurship is not just a way of creating a business, it's also a powerful school of life that helps build confidence. By taking risks and stepping out of their comfort zone, young entrepreneurs discover a source of confidence they may not have known they had.

Business is an area where risk-taking is inevitable. Whether it's launching a new product idea or conquering a new market, every decision involves an element of uncertainty. By confronting these uncertainties, we learn to master risk-taking, an essential skill in any entrepreneurial adventure.

When we succeed in turning our ideas into successful businesses, we feel a special sense of satisfaction. This personal success is a source of pride and strengthens our confidence in our abilities. "If I succeed, what can I do next? " becomes a new mentality. Imagine a complicated puzzle you've solved. Entrepreneurship is comparable to solving a gigantic real-life puzzle, each piece of which represents a step towards success.

Entrepreneurship cannot avoid failure, but it is in these moments that confidence is built. Entrepreneurs learn that every failure is a lesson, not an end. The ability to bounce back from failure is an important skill that goes far beyond business and applies to all aspects of life. Let's say you're playing a difficult video game and you lose at a certain level. Instead of giving up, you come back to the starting point, ready to overcome the obstacle. Entrepreneurship is a kind of game, but with real stakes.

Entrepreneurship teaches us to trust our own judgment and have confidence in our ideas. Not to constantly seek the approval of others, but to develop our confidence on the basis of our own experiences and successes. It's like a superhero suddenly discovering his powers and learning to master them. Entrepreneurship is about discovering your own superpowers and learning how to use them to achieve extraordinary things.

> Entrepreneurship acts as a catalyst, transforming teenagers into confident entrepreneurs, ready to face life's challenges with confidence. Every success and failure shapes not only the company, but also the person they will become. Get ready to discover the power of self-confidence that entrepreneurship can unleash in you.

Acquiring professional skills

Entrepreneurship is not just a business experience; it's a school of life where you acquire essential professional skills, tools that will serve not only to create businesses, but also to successfully meet the challenges of professional and personal life.

Entrepreneurship teaches us to manage the many facets of professional life, to set priorities and meet deadlines. Effective time management becomes a valuable skill, because every minute counts in the business world.

Entrepreneurs quickly learn to make informed decisions. Choosing the right path can be the key to success, while hasty decisions can lead to unexpected difficulties. This skill is invaluable, as it applies to all aspects of life.

Entrepreneurship puts us at the heart of exchanges with potential partners, customers and employees. The ability to communicate effectively becomes a key skill in building strong relationships and moving projects forward.

Learning to manage income and expenses and to understand the financial aspects of a business is a skill that entrepreneurship offers young people. This mastery of finances becomes a major asset in both personal and professional life. It's like having a certain budget for a party.

In the business world, negotiation is an essential skill. Entrepreneurs learn to find win-win solutions, to persuade and to conclude advantageous agreements. This skill extends beyond the world of business to become a powerful tool in all areas of life.

> Entrepreneurship is a practical school where we acquire a set of fundamental professional skills. These skills become versatile tools that are not only useful for starting a business, but accompany us throughout our professional career, whatever path we choose. Get ready to become an accomplished professional thanks to the skills that entrepreneurship will bring you.

Problem-solving capabilities

Entrepreneurship offers much more than just an opportunity to set up a business; it's a dynamic workshop where we tackle real-life problems and find innovative solutions. This experience transforms us into agile experts, armed with creativity and a sharp critical mind.

Entrepreneurship often begins with observing the world around us. Teenagers are taught to identify the problems and challenges of everyday life, both large and small. This sense of observation becomes a superpower, enabling us to find opportunities where others see problems. Like a detective solving puzzles in a video game, but with real problems to solve.

Entrepreneurship encourages critical thinking. Assess situations, analyze market needs and challenge the status quo. This critical thinking becomes a torch that lights the way to innovative solutions. Like a character in a spy movie that has to analyze clues to solve a mystery.

After identifying problems, entrepreneurship is about creating innovative solutions. Learning to think outside the box, exploring unconventional ideas and transforming concepts into real answers to challenges.

By finding solutions to concrete problems, the young entrepreneur discovers that failure is an integral part of the process. Each unsuccessful attempt becomes a valuable lesson that guides us towards more effective solutions. This ability to learn from failure and adapt is a fundamental skill for overcoming obstacles.

> Entrepreneurship is a playground where you become an inventor and problem-solver. It's a laboratory of innovation where challenges are not insurmountable obstacles, but opportunities to create something new and meaningful. Get ready to become a true solution architect through entrepreneurship.

Preparing for the future

Learning to be entrepreneurial from an early age is more than just a skill - it's a real preparation for a professional future. By cultivating these skills, we forge a path that prepares us to successfully evolve in the business world, whether by setting up our own company or making a significant contribution to an existing one.

Learning about entrepreneurship as a teenager opens the door to the possibility of setting up your own business. The skills acquired in time management, decision-making, communication, financial management and problem-solving become invaluable tools for setting up and developing a business. Even for those who don't choose to set up their own business, entrepreneurial skills are major assets. Teenagers can make a considerable contribution to an existing business by using their creativity, critical thinking and practical skills to solve problems and innovate.

Entrepreneurship teaches flexibility and adaptability, crucial qualities in a constantly changing professional world. We learn to adapt to change, seize new opportunities and turn challenges into levers for growth.

The world of entrepreneurship is a constant learning journey. We learn to constantly seek out new information, keep abreast of the latest trends and constantly develop our skills. This commitment to lifelong learning becomes an invaluable asset for personal and professional development.

The advantages of becoming an entrepreneur at a young age

Becoming an entrepreneur at an early age has many advantages for teenagers. Here are a few of the most significant:

Becoming an entrepreneur at a young age offers a unique opportunity to develop a set of practical skills that will become solid pillars for future success. By immersing themselves in the business world from an early age, young entrepreneurs acquire early skills that set them apart and prepare them for lasting success.

Entrepreneurship at an early age is more than just starting a business; it's a path to autonomy and independence. Teenagers who embrace the entrepreneurial spirit discover a unique freedom, make crucial decisions and take responsibility for their own destiny. The benefits of this autonomy extend far beyond the boundaries of their company, leaving a lasting imprint on their self-confidence and perception of personal achievement.

The decision to become an entrepreneur at a very young age opens the door to exceptional financial opportunities. Beyond simply starting a business, young entrepreneurs embark on a journey where they learn not only how to manage money, but also how to develop a regular source of income and plan wisely for the future. They also have the opportunity to explore and pursue their personal passions and interests. Personal fulfillment becomes the key to their entrepreneurial journey, improving not only their professional lives, but their general well-being too.

Examples of successful teenage entrepreneurs:

- Moziah Bridges - Mo's Bows

Moziah Bridges, at the age of nine, launched "Mo's Bows", a business creating handmade bow ties. Her passion for fashion inspired her to turn her creative talent into a thriving business. Today, Mo's Bows is a thriving business offering a variety of fashion products.

- Isabel and Caroline Bercaw - Da Bomb Bath Fizzers

At the age of ten and eleven, sisters Isabel and Caroline Bercaw created "Da Bomb Bath Fizzers", a company specializing in bath bombs. Their idea was inspired by their love of fun bath products.

Today, their company is a success, offering handcrafted bath products worldwide.

- Cory Nieves - Biscuits de M. Cory

At just six years old, Cory Nieves started selling cookies. Inspired by his passion for baking, he founded "Mr. Cory's Cookies". His business grew quickly, and Cory became a successful entrepreneur. His cookies are now famous, and he continues to be involved in philanthropic projects.

- Mark Zuckerberg - Co-founder of Facebook

Mark Zuckerberg launched Facebook from his university dorm room at the age of 19. What began as a project has become one of the world's most influential social networks. His story is a testament to the power of innovation and entrepreneurship, even at a young age.

- Farrah Gray - Entrepreneur and Author

Farrah Gray grew up in a tough Chicago neighborhood, but that didn't stop him from becoming a millionaire at the age of 14. He founded Far Out Food, Inc. a food distribution company. Today, he's a successful entrepreneur and acclaimed author.

- Ashley Qualls - Whateverlife.com

At the age of 17, Ashley Qualls launched "Whateverlife.com", a website offering free layouts for MySpace profiles. Her business quickly became a success, generating significant revenue from advertising. Ashley is an example of the power of personal initiative at a young age.

These real-life stories of teenage entrepreneurs and young professionals who have succeeded in building empires testify to the possibility of turning dreams into reality from an early age. Their journeys illustrate the value of teenage entrepreneurship, and show that with creativity, determination and perseverance, extraordinary things can be achieved. By following in their footsteps, young entrepreneurs can find the inspiration and motivation they need to embark on their own entrepreneurial adventure.

For you, the young entrepreneur of tomorrow, it's no longer words on paper; it's the beginning of the adventure, where your ideas come to life. In this first chapter, we'll cover the basics of entrepreneurship. We'll talk about the benefits, opportunities and skills you'll acquire along the way. Prepare to savor every page, as we take you on a journey of inspiration, learning and game-changing advice. Let's start with a journey that promises to transform you. The adventure begins now.

Part 1

The basics of entrepreneurship

What is entrepreneurship?

Entrepreneurship is first and foremost the process of designing, managing and developing a business. Simply put, you are the creator and conductor of your own project. In concrete terms, this means creating original ideas, gathering the necessary resources, taking calculated risks and mastering the financial aspects to ensure the smooth running of the business.

It's all about the birth of a vision. It all starts with an idea that resonates with you, prompting you to say: "There's something here worth exploiting". Then it's a game of construction, putting together the essential pieces of the puzzle - be they financial, material or human - to bring that idea to life.

The risk aspect is inevitable in the business world. It's like an artistic journey where you explore new territories. But here, instead of canvases, we manipulate concepts, markets and opportunities. All the while accepting that failure can be a necessary step towards success.

Financial management, often considered a domain reserved for experts, is in fact an essential skill. It's about understanding how every penny flows, how to invest it wisely, and how to use the numbers to fuel your project's growth.

> **Entrepreneurship is an intellectual and practical adventure in which you become the architect of your professional destiny.**

What is a start-up?

So, you've often heard the term "start-up" used, but what does it really mean and how does it differ from an ordinary company?

A start-up is much more than a company: it's a way of life, a state of mind, a way of operating focused on innovation. In simple terms, a start-up is a young company venturing into a new sector of activity, often characterized by strong growth, a constant search for new ideas and a quest for innovation.

A start-up is distinguished by its penchant for innovation. It often seeks to introduce something new to the market, whether it's a product, a service or an innovative way of solving a problem. Unlike traditional companies, start-ups often aim for rapid, significant growth. It can grow from a small team to an extensive organization in a relatively short space of time.

Young companies embrace change with enthusiasm. They are ready to quickly adapt their strategies, products and even their business model in response to market feedback. Because of their fast-growth nature, they frequently seek external financing, whether from investors, venture capital funds or other sources.

Advice for future entrepreneurs :

Be innovative: A successful business is often based on an innovative idea. You have to constantly look for new and creative ways to solve problems.

Innovation enables a start-up to stand out from the competition. By offering something new and different, a start-up can attract the attention of potential customers and position itself as an innovative alternative in the marketplace. Markets are constantly evolving and consumer needs are changing. Innovative start-ups are better equipped to identify these changes and quickly adapt their products or services to market needs.

Innovations create value, whether by improving process efficiency, offering unique functionalities or providing solutions to specific problems. This creation of value is often a determining factor in a start-up's success.

Investors are often interested in young, innovative companies with high growth rates. Innovation can enhance a company's credibility and attract financial interest.

The business world is characterized by evolution, and innovation gives a start-up the ability to adapt quickly. An innovative company is better able to adjust its strategies in line with market trends and user feedback.

Sometimes, innovation goes beyond simply improving existing products to create entirely new markets. This opens up unique prospects for growth and success.

Understanding your audience: Innovation is only valuable if it meets market needs. It's important to understand your potential users in depth and adapt your offering accordingly.

Understanding the audience enables a start-up to accurately identify the needs, problems and desires of the market. This approach is the basis for developing products or services that truly meet customers' needs. A start-up that understands its audience can adapt its offerings according to user preferences and feedback. This ensures that products or services remain relevant and attractive to the target audience.

By understanding the audience's specific needs, a start-up can create customized solutions that deliver real added value. This strengthens customer relationships and fosters long-term loyalty. It facilitates effective communication. A start-up can tailor its message to better reach its target audience, using language, channels and visuals that match their expectations.

Start-ups that understand their audience are better equipped to build strong relationships with their customers. This goes beyond the simple business transaction, creating an emotional bond that fosters trust and loyalty.

In-depth knowledge of the audience helps avoid the costly mistakes associated with launching products or services that don't meet market expectations. This reduces financial risk and improves the chances of success.

The best innovations are often born of an in-depth understanding of user needs. By placing the public at the center of the innovation process, a start-up can develop game-changing solutions. A company focused on customer satisfaction can positively differentiate itself from the competition. Customer satisfaction is essential to generate positive recommendations, which in turn contribute to the company's prosperity.

Be ready to change course: The road to success for a start-up is not always linear. So it's important to be ready to adjust your strategy, or even change direction if necessary.

Market conditions are constantly changing. Being ready for change means that the start-up is able to adapt quickly to changing trends, consumer preferences and competitive innovations.

Experience in the field can reveal crucial information that founders could not have foreseen at the outset. By being open to change, entrepreneurs are ready to quickly learn from their experience and adapt their business model accordingly. User feedback may indicate that adjustments are needed to optimize the product or service. Being ready to adapt enables the start-up to implement these adjustments pre-emptively, improving customer satisfaction.

Not all ideas produce the results we hope for, and pursuing a strategy that doesn't work can lead to a waste of valuable resources. Being prepared to make changes allows you to react constructively to failures. Rather than persisting with an approach that doesn't deliver the desired results, entrepreneurs can adjust their focus to maximize the chances of success and quickly align themselves with changing needs, ensuring that their product or service remains relevant and in demand.

Building a strong network: Relationships are vital in the business world. Connecting with other entrepreneurs, seeking out mentors and building a network can be a real source of advice and opportunities.

A well-established network provides invaluable access to the resources needed to develop a young company, whether in terms of financing, talent, advice or strategic partnerships. A network allows you to benefit from the experience of mentors and industry experts. These experienced advisors can guide entrepreneurs, offering valuable information and practical advice.

Potential investors, sponsors and financial partners often gravitate around entrepreneurial networks. A strong network can facilitate access to sources of funding crucial to the launch and growth of the company. Building relationships within the industry can lead to strategic partnerships. These alliances can open new doors, raise the profile of the start-up and facilitate the company's growth.

Follow-up from peers and professionals within the network can help validate the business idea. This recognition can boost founders' confidence and provide valuable information for refining the concept.

Recruiting talent is often a major challenge for young companies. An extensive network can be a source for recruiting skilled people who share the company's vision and are ready to contribute to its success.

Belonging to a network offers increased visibility. Peer recommendations and strong connections can form the basis of a start-up's marketing strategy and reinforce its credibility. Creating and developing a business can sometimes be a lonely experience. A network offers a community that understands the challenges and successes of entrepreneurship, reducing the feeling of isolation.

An active network provides real-time information on market trends, emerging opportunities and competitive developments. This enables the company to rapidly adapt its strategy to the changing business environment.

Learning from failure: Failure is often an inevitable stage in the world of entrepreneurship. You have to learn from your mistakes, put things right and move forward with greater wisdom.

Failures offer a unique opportunity for in-depth analysis of the business model. By understanding the reasons for failure, founders can make essential adjustments to their initial idea, thereby improving its viability. Learning to overcome failure strengthens an entrepreneur's resilience and prepares him or her to face future challenges with determination and perseverance.

Failures often highlight weaknesses in a company's operational structure, management or strategy. By identifying these weaknesses, significant improvements can be made to avoid the same mistakes in the future. By understanding these mistakes, founders can optimize the company's internal processes. This includes operations management, the supply chain, customer service and other key aspects that may have contributed to the company's failure.

Failure is a valuable source of experience. Lessons learned from failure can be more rewarding than successes, as they provide practical, tangible information on how to operate in the business world. Overcoming failure often requires the development of personal skills such as stress management, decision-making under pressure and effective communication. These skills are essential for any entrepreneur.

Failure can also indicate a mismatch between the company's offering and the real needs of the market. By learning from market reactions, entrepreneurs can adjust their strategy to better meet public demand.

Encouraging a learning culture within the team is fundamental. When company members see failure as a learning opportunity, it creates an environment where innovation and continuous improvement are valued. Learning from failure helps avoid repeating the same mistakes. This saves time and resources, strengthening the company's ability to make sustainable progress.

> A company is a daring adventure that combines creativity, innovation and the constant quest for growth. If you want to enter this world, arm yourself with passion, an open mind and a willingness to learn along the way.

Company classification

Choosing the right type of business is like navigating a sea of opportunity. Each path has its own characteristics, and understanding the nuances is essential to making an informed decision.

The retail trade

In retail, you'll be right at the heart of the action, whether you're selling fashionable clothes in a physical store or offering a carefully chosen selection of books in an online bookshop. This category covers all businesses that supply goods directly to consumers. Whether through in-store shelves or an online interface, you'll have the opportunity to see for yourself the impact your products have on customers.

Let's say you decide to open a clothing boutique. Shimmering racks of different outfits, enthusiastic fittings and personalized advice are all part of your daily routine. Or maybe you'd prefer to run an online bookshop, creating a digital space where book lovers can immerse themselves in imaginary worlds. In both cases, you're on the front line, responding to customers' needs and desires.

Challenges and benefits :

Retail offers unique proximity to consumers, but it can also present challenges, such as inventory management and consistent customer satisfaction. However, the benefits are many. The expression of joy when a customer finds the perfect product or the feeling of contributing to the local community can be gratifying experiences.

Whether you choose to sell physical products in a physical or virtual space, retail is an exciting adventure where you have the power to positively influence people's lives through what you offer. So dive into the world of retail with passion and creativity!

Technology and innovation

Getting involved in technology and innovation means diving into a world where the possibilities are as vast as the digital space itself. Maybe you're developing revolutionary mobile apps that make everyday life easier, or creating software that solves complex problems. Perhaps you have an idea for an innovative product that will change the game in the marketplace. In this field, imagination is your only limit.

Challenges and benefits :

Working in technology and innovation can be demanding, but the rewards are well worth the challenges. You'll have the opportunity to push the boundaries of creativity, solve complex technical problems and be at the forefront of technological advances. The feeling of accomplishment when an idea becomes reality is priceless.

Whether you decide to code lines that will change the world or create products that will define the future, technology and innovation pave the way for a world where every idea counts. So, young entrepreneur, arm yourself with your technological know-how and get ready to shape the future!

Services

Services represent a unique facet of the business world, showcasing what you do best. Here, you don't need to produce material objects, because it's your expertise, creativity or skills that are the real commodity. Whether you choose to advise, create or teach, you'll be selling the invisible, but the impact of your services will be real.

Let's say you have specialized skills in a particular field. You could become a consultant and offer your advice to other companies or individuals. If you have a talented pen, freelance writing could be your niche. In the service sector, your skills are your most valuable tool.

Challenges and benefits :

Working in services can be challenging, but it's also an opportunity to show your true worth. Your success will depend on the quality of your skills and the way you present them to the world. The rewards can be enormous, both financially and in terms of personal fulfillment, as you offer something unique and valuable.

Whether it's becoming a sought-after consultant or unleashing your creativity in a variety of services, this entrepreneurial field lets you turn your skills into the driving force behind your success. Get ready to turn your talents into lucrative opportunities and leave a unique mark on the business world!

Hospitality

Hospitality covers everything that revolves around the art of welcoming guests and creating masterful moments. Whether in a restaurant, café, hotel or even a catering business, the aim is to offer not only exceptional service, but also a unique experience. Here, you'll be the creator of memories, the master of ambiance and the architect of unforgettable moments.

Let's say you're passionate about cooking and love a friendly atmosphere. You could open your own café, offering people a space where they can relax and enjoy delicious culinary creations. Or perhaps start a catering business, bringing a special touch to the important events in people's lives. In the hospitality world, every detail counts to create a unique experience.

Challenges and advantages :

Working in the hospitality industry can be challenging, but also incredibly rewarding. The satisfaction of seeing people enjoy what you've created, the loyalty of satisfied customers and the opportunity to leave a lasting impression are among the unique rewards of this sector. Managing staff, maintaining high standards and dealing with seasonal changes are all challenges, but with the right approach, these challenges can be turned into opportunities for growth.

Get ready, young entrepreneur, to dive into the exciting world of hospitality, where you'll have the opportunity to create exceptional experiences and leave a positive mark on the lives of those you serve. Whether you're opening a cozy little café or a thriving catering business, you'll be at the heart of creating memorable moments.

Online business

Online business focuses on digital activities, from online sales to digital marketing. A field where you'll be at the heart of the digital revolution, using the power of the internet to reach a global audience. Whether you want to set up an online store to sell unique products or become an influencer who shares his or her passion with the world, this field offers an infinite canvas for digital creativity.

You have a passion for fashion and a talent for creating unique styles. You could launch your own online boutique, selling original items and sharing your lifestyle with customers from all over the world. Or maybe you're passionate about a specific topic, like technology or lifestyle, and want to share your ideas with the world. By becoming an influencer, you can create an online community around your passions.

Challenges and advantages :

Working in the e-commerce sector offers exceptional flexibility, but it's not without its challenges. Competition can be intense, and it's essential to keep abreast of the latest digital trends. However, the benefits are manifold. The ability to reach a global audience, work from anywhere and see the impact of your work first-hand are all unique aspects of this sector.

Get ready to explore the exciting world of online commerce, where every idea, every message and every transaction can become a piece of the digital puzzle you're creating. Whether you're becoming an e-commerce entrepreneur or developing your online presence as an influencer, the digital world belongs to you.

Franchises

Franchising involves taking over a proven business model. Rather than starting from scratch with an original idea, the franchisee joins an existing business. This means you run your own business, while benefiting from the support, training and reputation of the parent brand. Franchises can be found in a wide range of sectors, from fast food to services, giving budding entrepreneurs a wide variety of options.

If you're passionate about food and dream of opening a restaurant, you could choose to open a well-known fast-food franchise. Instead of creating a new brand, you could opt to open a franchise. You'll benefit from a recognized business model, the brand's reputation and the ongoing support of the parent company.

Benefits and responsibilities :

There are many advantages to opting for a franchise. You benefit from the proven success of the brand, initial and ongoing training, and access to shared resources. However, with this comes responsibility. As a franchisee, you must respect the parent company's standards and pay regular franchise fees.

The world of franchising offers the opportunity to run your own business while benefiting from the credibility and experience of an established brand. Whether you're thinking of opening a fast food, service or retail franchise, this model could be the key to realizing your entrepreneurial dreams.

Production

Production encompasses the manufacture of material goods. This is where dreams take shape, where imagination is translated into products that people can touch, feel and use. Production offers an infinite range of possibilities for creative entrepreneurs, whether launching a unique clothing line, creating handcrafted objects or manufacturing innovative products.

Do you have a passion for fashion and dream of launching your own clothing line? On the production side, you could work with designers, fabric manufacturers and artisans to bring your creations to life. Creating an artisanal brand is another route, allowing you to produce hand-made items with an emphasis on authenticity and originality.

Benefits and challenges :

Opting for production offers the satisfaction of seeing your ideas take shape in the form of physical products. However, this choice comes with certain challenges, such as managing production costs, finding reliable suppliers and guaranteeing a high level of quality. However, for those who want to make a tangible contribution to the world, the production sector offers a rewarding entrepreneurial adventure.

The world of production, where your ideas come to life in the form of physical products. Whether you're creating stylish garments or one-of-a-kind handmade pieces, production gives you the opportunity to make your mark on the material world around you.

Dear budding young entrepreneur, the world of business offers you a wide range of possibilities, each with its own advantages and challenges. With so many choices, how do you choose the path that's right for you? Here's some sound advice to help you explore this exciting path:

1. Follow your passions: When it comes to entrepreneurship, it's essential to choose a field that thrills and stimulates you. Explore your deepest passions, because that's where your energy and motivation lie. If you're interested in technology, consider areas such as app development or innovative product design. If creativity in clothing is your passion, garment production could be your path.

2. Identify your talents: Look at yourself in the mirror of your skills. What are the things you do with ease, which comes naturally to you? Identifying your talents will guide you to a field where you can excel. If you're a communications whiz, marketing or digital services could be your playground. If organization is your forte, operations management could be for you.

3. Balancing passion and profitability: While it's essential to follow your passions, it's also important to ensure the financial viability of your business. Look for a balance between what you're passionate about and what can generate income. Finding that happy medium is the key to keeping you motivated while ensuring the sustainability of your business.

4. Explore before you commit: Don't rush. Take the time to explore the different avenues of entrepreneurship. Ask around, try out ideas, maybe even do some internships in areas that interest you. The more you explore, the more you'll understand what really suits you.

5. Learn from the experience of others: Don't hesitate to look for examples of successful entrepreneurs in different fields. Understanding their backgrounds can be a source of inspiration and valuable information.

6. Remains open to change: Entrepreneurship is an evolutionary journey. Being open to change and adjustment is a necessity. Sometimes, the path you choose at the outset will change over time. Stay flexible and ready to adjust your trajectory.

> So, young entrepreneur, choose your path carefully, guided by your passions, nurtured by your talents, and don't be afraid to embark on this adventure that will open up infinite prospects for you. Good luck to you!

Different types of company

When it comes to business, there's no one-size-fits-all model. It's like choosing the style of music that suits you best. So let's talk about the main types of business:

1. Sole proprietorship

A sole proprietorship is a legal form of business in which a single person is responsible for all the company's activities. In other words, the owner and the company are not legally separate entities. This means that the owner is personally liable for the company's debts and obligations.

Here are some key features of a sole proprietorship:

Sole ownership: There is only one owner, who is responsible for the management and operations of the business.

Unlimited liability: The owner is personally liable for the company's debts. This means that if the business cannot repay its debts, the owner can be held liable and involve his or her personal assets in the repayment.

Administrative simplicity: The administrative formalities involved in setting up and running a sole proprietorship are generally less complicated than for other legal forms of business, such as companies.

Simplified taxation: Income from a sole proprietorship is generally reported on the owner's personal tax return. There is no tax separation between the business and the owner.

Flexibility: The owner has total control over decision-making and business management.

2. Auto-entrepreneur (Micro-entrepreneur)

The auto-entrepreneur, also known as micro-entrepreneur, is a simplified status for individual entrepreneurs wishing to set up and run a small business. It is designed to simplify administrative, tax and social security procedures, making it easier to launch an entrepreneurial activity, particularly for small businesses and the self-employed. Here are the main features of the auto-entrepreneur status:

Administrative simplicity: One of the main advantages of this system is the simplification of administrative formalities. Auto-entrepreneurs benefit from streamlined accounting and simplified procedures for declaring and paying social security contributions and taxes.

Simplified taxation: Auto-entrepreneurs pay income tax based on their sales, with a fixed rate determined by their activity. There is no VAT to be levied on services provided by auto-entrepreneurs, but for commercial activities, the VAT exemption applies up to a certain sales threshold.

Limited liability: unlike sole proprietorships, auto-entrepreneurs benefit from limited liability, which means that their liability is generally limited to the amount of their sales.

Sales ceilings: The auto-entrepreneur status is subject to annual sales ceilings. If sales exceed these thresholds, the entrepreneur may have to opt for another status, such as micro-enterprise or the classic sole proprietorship.

Business sectors: The auto-entrepreneur scheme is open to a wide variety of business sectors, from services and commercial activities to crafts and liberal professions.

It should be noted that auto-entrepreneur status may vary from country to country, and specific benefits may differ according to local regulations. Before choosing this status, it is advisable to consult the relevant tax authorities and organizations to understand the specifics of the regime in your region.

3. Corporation

A corporation, also known as a joint-stock company, is a legal form of business that is a separate and distinct entity from its owners. Key features of a corporation include:

Separate legal personality: A corporation is considered a separate legal entity from its shareholders (owners). This means that the corporation can hold assets, sign contracts and be sued as a separate entity (legal person).

Limited liability: Shareholders of a corporation have limited liability, which means that their financial responsibility is generally limited to the amount invested in the company's shares. Shareholders' personal assets are generally not involved in covering the company's debts.

Share issue: A stock corporation can raise funds by issuing shares, which represent ownership in the company. Shareholders hold shares according to their investment in the company.

Board of Directors: Corporations are managed by a Board of Directors elected by the shareholders. The Board of Directors makes important decisions for the company, and usually appoints senior executives, such as the President and Chief Executive Officer (CEO).

Perpetual lifespan: A company's lifespan is generally unlimited, regardless of the lifespan of its shareholders. Shares can be transferred to other parties, facilitating continuity of operations.

Separate taxation: Corporations are generally taxed separately from their shareholders. They pay taxes on their income, while shareholders pay taxes on the salaries and dividends they receive.

Dividends are periodic payments made by a company to its shareholders, generally in proportion to the number of shares they hold. These payments represent a share of the company's profits distributed to shareholders in return for their investment in the company. Dividends may be paid quarterly, semi-annually or annually, depending on the company's distribution policy.

> This type of company is generally chosen by large-scale enterprises because of its complex structure and the possibility of raising funds on the financial markets by issuing shares. It also offers considerable protection against the personal liability of shareholders.

4. Limited liability company (LLC)

The LLC is neither a joint-stock company nor a sole proprietorship. The LLC is a legal form of enterprise that shares certain characteristics with both, but differs in a number of important respects.

Here are some key distinctions between an LLC and a corporation:

Limited liability: As with corporations, shareholders of an LLC also benefit from limited liability, meaning that their financial responsibility is generally limited to the amount of their investment.

Number of shareholders: LLCs are generally designed to be medium-sized companies, and often have a limited number of shareholders. In many countries, the number of shareholders in an LLC is also limited by law.

Governance structure: While corporations are generally managed by a board of directors elected by shareholders, LLCs generally have a more flexible governance structure. The shareholders of an LLC may participate directly in the day-to-day running of the company, or delegate this responsibility to managers.

Transferability of shares: Shares in a corporation are generally more easily transferable than shares in an LLC. LLCs often have restrictions on the transfer of shares in order to maintain tighter control over the composition of their capital.

Lifespan: LLCs can have a limited lifespan specified in their articles, while corporations generally have an unlimited lifespan.

> Although the LLC and the corporation share certain similarities, they are distinct legal forms, each with its own advantages and disadvantages. The choice between an LLC and a corporation often depends on the size of the business, the nature of its activities and the specific objectives of its managers.

The LLC is not a sole proprietorship. A sole proprietorship is a structure in which a single person owns the business and is responsible for all its activities. The LLC, on the other hand, is a form of company in which at least two associates (natural or legal persons), called partners or shareholders, hold shares in the company.

Here are some of the major differences between a sole proprietorship and an LLC:

Number of owners: A sole proprietorship has a single owner, while an LLC has at least two partners. These partners may be natural or legal persons.

Liability: In a sole proprietorship, the owner has unlimited liability, meaning that he or she is personally responsible for the company's debts. In an LLC, on the other hand, the liability of the partners is generally limited to the amount of their investment in the company.

Management structure: In a sole proprietorship, the owner generally makes all decisions and manages the business autonomously. In an LLC, management can be delegated to a designated manager, and important decisions can be taken collectively by the partners.

Formalities for setting up a sole proprietorship: Formalities for setting up a sole proprietorship are often simpler than those for a limited liability company, which require the definition of articles of association, the appointment of managing directors, and so on.

> The LLC is a form of company that offers a degree of separation between the partners' personal capital and the company's debts, which distinguishes it from both the sole proprietorship (with unlimited liability) and the joint-stock company (which generally has a larger number of shareholders).

Now, why on earth is any of this important to you, budding young entrepreneur? Because choosing the right type of business depends on your vision, your way of working, and how you want to share the burden (and the success!).

What's best for you? Being the sole captain of your ship, joining forces with other players, or creating an entity with an autonomous legal existence? The choice is yours, and it's one of the first exciting decisions you'll have to make in the exciting world of business creation, which will be the subject of the next chapter.

Starting a business

Once you've taken a short tour of the business world, with its sole proprietorships, LLCs and corporations, it's time, as an ambitious young person, to take the next step: creating your own entrepreneurial adventure.

Creating a company is a bit like sculpting a statue from a simple block of marble. You start with a raw idea and, through a technical process, sculpt, polish and bring it to life. Here's how the process takes shape:

Market research

Imagine you're a detective, but instead of solving puzzles, you're trying to understand your market. Who are your potential customers? What makes them dream? Who are your competitors? This step enables you to identify opportunities and understand how to make your unique creation stand out in the business world.

- **Customer profile**

Who are your potential customers? Define their demographics, preferences and buying behaviors. It's more than just data; it's a detailed portrait of the person for whom your product is designed.

- **Motivation analysis**

Whether it's a product or a service, it's essential to understand what motivates your customers. What makes them buy? What needs or desires are they looking to fulfill? This in-depth understanding guides the way you position your offering in the marketplace.

- **Competitive analysis**

Let's face it: you're not alone in the field. Who are your direct and indirect competitors? What are their strengths and weaknesses? Competitor analysis allows you to draw inspiration from their successes, while avoiding the mistakes they may have made.

- **Identifying opportunities**

Where there are challenges, there are also opportunities. By understanding your market in depth, you identify gaps, unmet needs and niches you could fill. That's when you determine how your service can stand out from the crowd.

- **Strategic positioning**

How do you want your audience to perceive you in relation to the competition? This is where you define your strategic positioning. You're not just another choice, you're the choice that stands out, that responds specifically to the needs and aspirations of your audience.

> Far from being a simple procedure, market research becomes an immersion in the world of your future customers and competitors. It's a strategic process that helps you define a clear vision of your company's place in the commercial landscape. So, young businessman, put on your detective hat and immerse yourself in the subtle nuances of your market. The answers you find will guide every decision you make.

Creating a business plan

Your business plan is like the map that guides you on your journey. It details your idea, your vision and how you plan to achieve your goals. It also includes financial estimates, to show that you've thought the budget through.

- **Corporate vision**

Every business plan begins with a thorough examination of the company's vision. What is your mission? What principles will guide your every decision? This is the foundation on which everything else will be built.

- **Strategic objectives**

It's essential to define clear, measurable objectives. Where do you want your company to be in one year, three years or even ten? These goals give a clear direction to your journey and serve as a compass to guide your actions.

- **Market analysis**

Drawing on the results of your investigation as a market detective, this section details how you position your product or service. How does it meet your identified needs? What's your added-value proposition?

- **Organizational structure**

Who does what? How is your team organized? This section reveals the company's internal structure and highlights the skills needed by each person to achieve the objectives set.

- **Financial plan**

The central part is not to be neglected. What are your financial needs? How do you plan the distribution of resources? The financial outlook shows that everything has been thought through, from the start-up phase through to future growth.

- **Marketing strategies**

What's your strategy for promoting your company? What are your tactics for attracting and retaining customers? This section explores communication channels and methods for effectively positioning the company in the marketplace. Here are a few tips:

Understand your audience: Before defining strategies, understand your potential customers. What motivates them? Where do they spend their time online? The more you know about them, the more targeted your strategies will be.

Impactful storytelling: Tell your company's story in a captivating way. People remember stories more than hard facts. Create a narrative that resonates with your values and creates an emotional connection.

Use social media to your advantage: Young people are often very active on social networks. Use these platforms strategically. Choose the ones that are most relevant to your audience and create engaging content.

Optimize your website: If you have a website, make sure it's user-friendly and optimized for search engines (SEO). This is often the first impression people have of your company.

Influencer collaborations: If it makes sense for your industry, consider collaborations with influencers who have an audience aligned with your products or services.

Promotions and special offers: Young people love a bargain. Offer special promotions or exclusive deals to attract attention and encourage purchases.

Involvement on visual platforms: Use visual platforms like Instagram, TikTok or Pinterest to visually show what your company has to offer. Visuals attract attention.

Feedback and responsiveness: Be attentive to your customers' feedback. Use it to adjust your marketing strategies. A company that listens is a company that evolves.

Community management: Create a community around your company. Young people are sensitive to brands that interact directly with them. Be present on social media to answer questions and create a sense of community.

Local events and activities: If possible, take part in local events or organize activities that put you in direct contact with your audience. Human contact can be very powerful.

Creative use of video: Videos are a powerful way to capture attention. Whether it's tutorials, brand stories, or funny videos, explore different ways to use video to broaden your company's impact.

Loyalty programs: Encourage loyalty by offering programs that reward regular customers. These may include discounts, exclusive privileges or gifts.

Internal influencer marketing: Your first customers can become your brand ambassadors. Encourage word-of-mouth and referrals by offering benefits to existing customers to encourage them to recommend your products or services.

Measure and adjust: Use analytical tools to measure the effectiveness of your strategies. Be ready to adapt according to the results.

Authenticity above all: customers appreciate authenticity. Be real in your communication. Don't try to be something you're not. Customers quickly detect sincerity and authenticity.

> The business plan is the centerpiece that gives shape to your dreams. It's your guide, your roadmap that explains how you're going to turn your idea into a commercial reality. It's an intellectual and pragmatic exercise that requires thought, foresight and a clear vision of the future. Ready to unfold your roadmap and follow the path you've mapped out? Good luck, ambitious young man.

Search for Financing

You don't have to be Croesus to start a business, but a little money can go a long way. Whether you're saving, borrowing from family and friends, or looking for investors, there are many ways to finance your vision. This is where you give substance to your dream.

- **Personal savings**

Starting with your own savings shows your commitment to your project. It shows that you believe in your idea enough to invest your own money. It's an act of self-confidence.

- **Family and friends**

The first step is often to borrow from family and friends. Initially, this source of financing can be more flexible and less bureaucratic. However, it is essential to treat these arrangements with the same rigor as with more formal investors.

- **Private investors**

If your project requires a larger injection of capital, you may want to consider private investors. These individuals or groups invest their money in projects they believe have a high potential return.

They often negotiate shares in the company in exchange for financing.

- **Loans and grants**

Financial organizations offer business loans, but it's important to carefully study the conditions and interest involved. On the other hand, there are government or association grants to support young entrepreneurs, which can be a considerable asset.

- **Participatory financing (crowdfunding):**

A more modern approach is crowdfunding. Online platforms allow you to solicit funds from a multitude of contributors. It's a way of validating your idea with a community while raising funds.

- **Venture capital**

If your project has strong growth and innovation potential, venture capital may be an option. Specialized companies invest large sums in exchange for significant shares in the company.

- **Alternative financing**

Explore other forms of financing, such as participatory corporate financing, revenue-based financing or profit-sharing agreements.

Key tips :

Prepare a solid plan: Whether you're convincing investors or applying for loans, a solid business plan is essential. Show that you've thought about all the financial aspects.

Diversify sources: Avoid putting all your eggs in one financial basket. Diversifying funding sources reduces risk.

Keep an eye on profitability: Financing is not an end in itself. Always keep in mind the profitability of your business and how it will repay or return profits to investors.

Be transparent: Whether it's your family, friends or investors, transparency is key. Be honest about risks and return prospects.

> The search for financing is an essential element in the realization of your vision. It's an art that requires strategy, prudence and a keen sense of opportunity and risk. Remember, each financing round is a step towards realizing your entrepreneurial dream.

Company registration

Now that you've got the idea, the plan and the money, it's time to give your project a legal existence. This is where the company becomes an official entity. You choose a name, fill out the necessary paperwork, and voila, your business is on the map.

- **Choice of company name**

Choosing the right name is more than a matter of personal preference. It's a strategic choice that reflects the company's identity and value proposition. It must be unique, memorable and compliant with registration regulations.

Availability search: Before you commit to a name, make sure it's available. Check that the domain name is available online, and that it has been registered with the appropriate authorities. This avoids legal complications and reinforces the consistency of your online presence.

Clarity and relevance: Choose a clear, relevant name that expresses the nature of your business. Avoid names that are too complex or difficult to pronounce. Clarity makes it easier to remember.

Memorability: A memorable name is an asset. It facilitates recognition and retention in the minds of potential customers. Avoid overly generic names that could get lost among others.

Avoids geographical restrictions: If you plan to expand beyond your current region, avoid names that are too specific to one geographical location. This allows your company to have a broader reach.

Consider the sound: The sound of the name is important, especially if you intend to use it regularly in a professional context. Make sure it sounds good and is pleasant to the ear.

Avoids negative connotations: You should also check that the name has no negative connotations in other languages or cultures. It would be a shame for your company name to be misinterpreted.

Long-term thinking: Think about the durability of the name. A name that works well in the start-up phase may not be suitable for a more mature business. Anticipate the evolution of your business.

Consult your audience: If possible, test the name with your target audience. Their perception can give you valuable information. Make sure it resonates positively with them.

Legal compliance: The name must comply with the registration and intellectual property rules in force in your country. Avoid legal risks by checking name availability and respecting existing rights.

Avoids passing trends: Trends can change very quickly. Avoid choosing a name based solely on a current trend, as it could become obsolete. Opt for a name that remains relevant over time.

Internet domain available: Make sure the associated domain name is available. A website matching a company's name strengthens its online presence.

Remains unique: Avoid choosing a name too similar to that of other companies, especially in the same field. Distinction is crucial to avoid confusion.

> Choosing a company name is a strategic decision. You need to take the time to choose a name that perfectly represents the company's vision and will stand the test of time. It's one of the first impressions the company will leave, so make sure it's memorable and positive.

- **Legal structure**

Determining the legal structure of your business is an important decision. Whether it's a sole proprietorship, a limited liability company (LLC) or a corporation (SA), each structure has different tax, legal and liability obligations, as we've already seen in previous chapters. Here again are the main points to consider when choosing a legal structure:

1. **Sole proprietorship**

Characteristics: A sole proprietorship is owned and operated by a single individual.

Implications: This is the simplest structure, but the owner is responsible for all debts and obligations. Profits are taxed at the personal level.

2. **Limited liability company (LLC)**

Features: An LLC offers limited liability to the owners (called partners). It combines the simplicity of a sole proprietorship with some legal protection.

Implications: Profits are often taxed at the partners' personal level, but personal liability is limited.

3. Joint stock company (SA)

Characteristics: A public limited company is a separate entity from its shareholders. Shares represent ownership.

Implications: It offers strong protection against personal liability. Profits are taxed at corporate level, but shareholders are also taxed on dividends.

4. Auto-entrepreneur (Micro-entrepreneur)

Features: A simplified option for sole traders with limited sales.

Implications: Taxation is simplified, but personal liability is total.

Tips for choosing a legal structure:

Risk assessment: Evaluate the risks associated with your business. If you foresee significant financial obligations, it's best to opt for a limited liability structure.

Long-term objectives: Consider your long-term goals. Certain types of structure are better suited to growth and expansion.

Administrative complexity: Weigh up the administrative complexity associated with each structure. Some require more formalities and regular reporting.

Taxation: Understand the tax implications of each structure. Some offer better tax optimization depending on expected income.

Number of associates: If you have partners, consider a structure that allows shared ownership while protecting personal liability.

Potential development: Choose a structure that can grow with your business. It can be expensive to change structures later on.

Professional consulting: Consulting an accounting or business law professional can provide advice tailored to your specific situation.

> The legal structure of a company is like the framework of a house: it supports everything else. So you need to take the time to assess all your needs, understand the implications of each option, and choose the structure that best suits your long-term vision.

- **Registration with the authorities**

Registration procedures vary according to the country and structure chosen. They generally involve filling in specific forms, paying registration fees and providing documents such as the company's articles of association. Registering your company is a bit like giving it a passport to the business world. It's a process which, while requiring a few formalities, gives the project a legal existence.

Start by choosing a name that reflects the essence of the company's activity. Once the name has been chosen, fill out a registration form. Registration often comes with a fee.

Obtaining a tax identification number is a bit like giving your company a social security number. Depending on the type of business, specific authorizations may be required. These may include appropriate licenses. If you plan to have an online presence, register the domain name corresponding to your company name. Obtaining a tax identification number is usually an essential step. This enables the company to be recognized by the tax authorities and facilitates the management of taxes.

Before getting started, you need to make sure that everything is in order. It's a bit like doing a final check before setting off on your adventure. Once you've taken all the necessary steps, you'll be issued with official documents such as registration certificates. As the business world evolves, so does the company. Don't forget to regularly update the information you have with the authorities. Every business structure is subject to specific compliance rules. These may include publication obligations, annual reports or other legal requirements. It's essential to be informed and to respect these rules.

- **Trademarks and patents**

If the company's activity is based on unique products or services, intellectual property protection becomes crucial. This may involve registering trademarks, patents or other intellectual property rights.

Trademarks

A trademark, also known simply as a "brand", is a distinctive sign that differentiates a company's products or services from those of others. It is an essential element of intellectual property and plays an important role in the marketing and legal protection of businesses. A trademark can take many forms, including names, logos, slogans, colors, shapes or even combinations of these elements.

Registration: Official protection is provided by registering these elements with the relevant authorities. By registering a trademark with authorities such as a country's intellectual property office, a company obtains the legal right to use the trademark for the products or services for which it is registered.

Patents

A patent is an exclusive right granted by the State to a person or company for a new and inventive invention. In other words, a patent provides its holder with a temporary monopoly on the exploitation of his or her invention, and prohibits others from making, using, selling or distributing that invention without authorization. Patents are a key element of the intellectual property protection system, and are generally granted by national patent offices.

The process: Obtaining a patent often requires a more complex procedure, during which the novelty, inventiveness and usefulness of the invention must be demonstrated in detail. To be eligible for a patent, an invention must be new, i.e. it must not have been previously disclosed to the public. It must also be inventive, which means that it must not be obvious to anyone skilled in the technical field.

To obtain a patent, the creator of the invention must file a patent application with the patent office. The application must describe the invention in detail and provide specific claims defining the unique aspects of the invention. Patents are generally granted at national level, which means that the inventor must file a patent application in each country where he or she wishes to obtain protection. There are also procedures, such as the European patent, which enable protection to be obtained in several European countries by filing a single application.

The owner of a patent has the exclusive right to exploit the invention, and may grant licenses to other parties to use the invention in exchange for remuneration. However, the owner also has an obligation to disclose details of the invention in the patent application, thus contributing to the company's technical knowledge base. Unlike trade secrets, the information contained in a patent application generally becomes public once the patent has been granted.

Patents have a limited duration, generally 20 years from the date of filing of the patent application. Once the period of protection has expired, the invention falls into the public domain, meaning that it becomes accessible to all.

Intellectual property rights

In addition to trademarks and patents, there are other forms of intellectual property rights, such as copyrights and trade secrets. Each is designed to protect different aspects of creativity and innovation.

Protection benefits

Exclusivity: Intellectual property protection guarantees exclusive rights to your own creations. This means that no one else can legally reproduce, use or sell your products or services without your consent.

Added value: This adds considerable value to the company's business. Registered trademarks and patents can increase the perceived value of products or services.

Before starting the registration process, it's essential to carry out thorough research to check that no one else has already registered something similar.

Intellectual property rights are not eternal. They must be renewed periodically to maintain their validity. It's a bit like insurance, which needs to be regularly updated.

> Understanding the ins and outs of intellectual property protection can be complex. It is often advisable to consult a lawyer specialized in intellectual property.

- **Opening a business bank account**

To keep personal and business finances separate, we recommend opening a business bank account in the company's name. This simplifies financial management and consolidates the company's credibility.

Opening a business bank account establishes a clear boundary between personal and business finances. It simplifies financial management by creating a dedicated structure for business transactions. In this way, the company's income, expenses and financial health are clearly identified. With a business account, you have access to specialized corporate banking services. These include lines of credit, payment solutions and other customized financial tools.

A business account facilitates transactions with customers, partners and suppliers. It also contributes to the company's image of credibility and professionalism.

Choosing the right bank is like choosing a trusted partner for your business. You need to consider the bank's services, fees and reputation.

- **Company insurance**

Consider insurance needs to protect the business against potential risks. This may include liability insurance, professional indemnity insurance or other types of insurance.

Before taking out insurance, it's essential to identify the company's specific needs. It's a bit like diagnosing the company's health.

Liability insurance

Liability insurance is like a shield that protects the company against claims for bodily injury or property damage caused to third parties. In the event of a dispute or accident, legal costs and compensation are paid by the insurance company, not by the company's finances.

Professional liability insurance

This insurance is specifically designed for professionals offering services. It covers errors, omissions or negligence that may occur in the course of professional activities. It's like double-checking to ensure that every service offered is impeccable.

Other relevant forms of insurance

Depending on the nature of the company's activities, other forms of insurance may be required. These may include property insurance, cyber insurance or other options tailored to specific activities.

Before choosing an insurance policy, it is essential to carry out a thorough analysis of the potential risks to which the company may be exposed. It's important to strike the right balance in terms of coverage levels. Too little insurance exposes the company to risk, while too much can put a strain on finances.

The terms and conditions of insurance policies can be complicated. Consulting an insurance expert can help you make informed decisions.

- **Retention of legal documents**

All legal documents must be carefully preserved, including contracts, articles of association, licenses and other official documents. This can be crucial in the event of a tax audit or other administrative proceedings.

Registering a company is a fundamental step in giving it a legal existence. It's a serious process that requires a thorough understanding of local regulations and rigorous management. It's about creating the solid foundations on which the business will thrive.

Setting up operations

Your company is no longer an idea on paper, it's a living entity. How will it function on a day-to-day basis? Who does what? How will products or services be created and distributed? It's time to put in place the mechanisms and cogs of your well-oiled machine.

- **Process definition**

It's time to clearly define operational processes. Who does what? How is each task performed?

Defining processes creates the company's operational structure. It's a bit like designing the detailed plans for a complex building, ensuring a solid foundation for growth.

Each defined process goes hand in hand with a clear allocation of responsibilities. Who does what? The answer to this question lies in the precise definition of each role within the company.

Defining processes also means determining the sequence of operations. It's a bit like writing the script for a play, where each act has its place in the whole. Each defined process must be consistent with the company's overall objectives.

Transparent processes promote effective communication between team members. It also helps identify areas for improvement.

Defining the process is like composing a symphony where each instrument plays in harmony to create a captivating work. Every detail is carefully noted, every actor knows when to come on stage, and the whole forms a performance that impresses and challenges. So think of the definition of the process as the score that guides every player in the company towards an outstanding performance.

The design of the organizational structure is a key element in the implementation of operations. It is the art of defining relationships and responsibilities within the company, creating a coherent hierarchy.

Stability: The organizational structure is the foundation on which the entire company rests. It's a bit like erecting the solid pillars of a building to ensure stability.

Strategic assignment: Each level of the hierarchy has specific responsibilities. It's a bit like the cast of a play, with each actor making a unique contribution to the plot.

Agility: Organizational structure determines the scale of decision-making. It's a bit like determining who holds the scepter of command in each act of the play.

Support: Higher hierarchical levels are often responsible for mentoring and supporting lower levels, enabling the company to develop in an organized way.

- **Supply chain management**

Fluidity: if your business involves the production of goods, supply chain management is crucial.

Supply chain management is the art of ensuring continuous fluidity in the production and distribution of goods within a company. It's a complex ballet in which every move counts. Here's an approach to this crucial step:

Consistency: Supply chain management must be aligned with the company's overall strategy, and work closely with suppliers.

Supply chain management involves meticulous planning of production, warehousing and logistics to ensure smooth distribution. Effective supply chain management aims to optimize costs. The integration of innovative technologies can play a crucial role in this.

Flexibility: The supply chain must be able to adapt to market changes. Anticipation and risk management are fundamental. It's a bit like having back-up solutions in place to ensure that a show runs smoothly despite the unexpected.

 Responsible supply chain management includes sustainable practices and continuous evaluation to enable constant fine-tuning.

- **Technology integration**

Modernity: Technology integration can play a key role in modernizing operations. It is the lever that propels a company's operations towards modernity. It's the art of adopting the most advanced tools to thrive in an ever-changing world.

Vision: every technological adoption must be in line with the company's strategic objectives. It's a bit like choosing the special effects that enhance the overall impact of a show.

Efficiency: Process automation aims to increase operational efficiency. Data analysis offers enlightening insights for decision-making.

Protection: Cybersecurity ensures that operations are protected from digital threats. It's a bit like having security guards behind the scenes. Artificial intelligence (AI) brings intelligent adaptability to processes. Training and the adoption of new technologies are essential. It's a bit like preparing actors to use new accessories to improve their performance.

Integrating technologies means equipping the company with a palette of futuristic tools to create a cutting-edge operational experience. Each technology adopted brings with it a host of new features that enrich the company's overall performance.

Staff training

Staff training is the key to sculpting operational expertise within the company. It's the art of imparting to each team member the skills needed to excel in their respective roles. Ensuring that staff are trained and competent is an integral part of setting up operations.

Assessment: Prior to training, a thorough assessment is carried out to identify the skills required. The assessment is a careful study of the terrain before building a solid foundation. This is the stage where every aspect of skills is carefully examined, measured and planned to ensure that the training that follows is perfectly geared to improving individual and collective skills. This assessment should be seen as the compass that guides the way to operational expertise.

The assessment starts with a careful mapping of each team member's current skills and potential gaps, and matches needs to skills. In addition to assessing skills, the assessment also anticipates future skills needs.

Training programs are carefully designed to cover all operational aspects; initial training prepares staff to enter the operational arena. Ongoing training aims to perfect skills over time. The use of appropriate teaching methods ensures effective transmission of knowledge. Encourage autonomous learning, enabling staff to take charge of their own progress.

- **Growth planning**

Planning for growth goes beyond day-to-day operations, and requires a strategic perspective and thoughtful anticipation of the future. It's an informed exploration of future horizons, aimed at positioning the company for sustainable success.

Planning for growth begins with a long-term strategic vision. Anticipating growth involves in-depth analysis of trends and the development of new markets, exploring new territories to broaden the company's influence.

The company carefully assesses its internal capabilities to determine its growth potential. Growth planning anticipates needs in terms of human, financial and technological resources.

Growth planning incorporates a culture of continuous development and innovation. Strategic investments aim to strengthen the company's positioning.

> **Setting up operations is like modelling a work of art that comes to life every time you engage with it. Each decision shapes the company's structure, giving it the ability to meet challenges and thrive in the business world. So consider, young entrepreneur, that each procedure is a note in the dynamic symphony of your success.**

Marketing your company

Once all the essential elements are in place, it's time to deploy the promotional arsenal and conquer the hearts of potential customers. This is not a simple advertising tactic, but a strategy in which every act contributes to the harmony of the brand's commercial presence. Let's dive into this crucial stage with a few practical tips:

- **Creation of a proven marketing strategy:**

 Developing a solid marketing strategy is the backbone of any promotional campaign. It's like composing symphonic music, where every note is designed to create a memorable experience.

- ✓ Before composing this music, getting into the head of your audience is an essential step. Understand their needs, their preferences and speak their language. The song must resonate with the audience's emotions.
- ✓ Don't treat everyone the same. Segmenting your audience allows you to adapt the tone and content of your communication. It's like tuning each note to create a personalized melody.
- ✓ Use multiple communication channels, while ensuring that the message remains the same.
- ✓ Whether on social networks, posters or advertisements, it's important to ensure that the brand image is consistent.
- ✓ Be active on social networks. Reply to comments, ask questions.
- ✓ Remain attentive to what others are doing.

- **Taking part in local events:**

Raising local awareness: Participating in local events is like playing live in front of an audience. It allows you to establish direct links with your community and leave a tangible mark.

Networking: Don't underestimate the power of networking. It's about forging links with other players on the local scene to mutually reinforce the company's presence.

Precise targeting: Launching advertising campaigns requires precise targeting. It's a bit like lighting up certain parts of the stage to draw attention exactly where you want it.

Creativity: Be creative in your advertising storytelling. It's a bit like writing punchy dialogue to capture attention and stimulate emotion.

Measuring results: Evaluate the effectiveness of your campaigns. It's a bit like getting feedback after a show, and adjusting your performance to maximize its impact.

- **Integration of a consistent brand image:**

Visual identity: Brand image is like a suit on the professional stage. It's important to ensure that this image is consistent across all media. It's a bit like maintaining a constant visual presence at every performance.

Brand story: Every company has a story. It needs to be shared in a captivating way, making the audience feel connected to that brand.

- **Exploiting social networks and digital technology :**

Continuous interaction: Social networks are your audience behind the scenes. Interact constantly to maintain engagement. It's a bit like chatting with the audience between performances to maintain enthusiasm.

Quality content: Digital content is like a script. It must be of impeccable quality. It's like writing scenes that captivate and inspire the audience.

- **Continuous adaptation to market developments:**

Readjustment: Always be ready to readjust your strategy as the market evolves.

Competitive intelligence: Always keep an eye on the competition. It's like watching the other players to understand how you can stand out from the crowd.

Retrospective: Reflect at the end of each campaign. It's a bit like a retrospective after a performance, where you analyze what worked and what can be improved.

> **Marketing your company is a continuous performance, where every initiative is a step that contributes to the company's success. Every campaign is a performance and an opportunity to captivate, inspire and seduce the public. Think of it as staging the company on the big stage of the business world.**

Available resources

In the vast adventure of entrepreneurship, every young pioneer needs his or her own arsenal. Let's talk about the resources that will be your allies in this quest for success.

- **Business incubators: Nurturing your idea**

Business incubators are real greenhouses for germinating ideas. These specialized centers offer an environment conducive to start-up growth. Experienced mentors, shared resources and a thriving network are at your disposal. Joining an incubator is like planting your seeds in fertile soil, with a constant sprinkling of sound advice and support.

- ✓ Don't be shy about asking for advice. Mentors are there to share their wisdom, but they can only do so if you're willing to listen.
- ✓ Take advantage of shared resources. Collaborate with other entrepreneurs. It's like exchanging seeds with the neighbor in your vegetable garden. Who knows what might sprout?
- ✓ Incubator events are golden opportunities. They're like the days when the head gardener gives practical advice. Be there, participate, learn.
- ✓ Don't limit your network to the incubator. Expand it. It's like planting seeds all over the garden. You never know where an opportunity will sprout.

Here are just a few examples of renowned incubators that have helped numerous start-ups grow and succeed:

Y Combinator: Based in California, Y Combinator is one of the world's best-known incubators. It offers seed funding, advice from leading mentors and a community of successful entrepreneurs.

Techstars: A global network of incubators offering acceleration programs in various sectors. They provide seed funding, mentors and workspace.

500 Startups: 500 Startups is a global incubator that invests in companies worldwide. It offers acceleration programs, financing and resources to help startups grow.

Seedcamp: Based in London, Seedcamp is a European incubator focusing on technology startups. They provide seed funding, mentoring and access to a global network.

Station F: Station F is the world's largest startup campus, located in Paris. It offers workspace, acceleration programs and a dynamic ecosystem for entrepreneurs.

Mass Challenge: Mass Challenge is a global not-for-profit incubator offering non-equity funding, mentors and resources to help startups succeed.

The Hatchery: The Hatchery is a New York-based incubator focusing on food and beverage companies. It offers financial support, specialized mentoring and access to industry resources.

Wagon: Le Wagon is not only an incubator, but also an intensive bootcamp for learning to code. It has helped train many of France's technology entrepreneurs.

Le Cargo Paris: Le Cargo Paris is an incubator dedicated to the cultural and creative industries. It offers workspaces, a mentoring program and networking opportunities.

Paris&Co : Paris&Co is an economic development and innovation agency that manages several incubators in Paris, covering sectors such as finance, healthcare and mobility.

The Family: The Family is an organization that supports entrepreneurs in Europe. They provide workspace, events and a strong network to help startups grow.

Bpifrance Le Hub: An innovation hub and incubator managed by Bpifrance, offering support to innovative startups in various sectors.

La Piscine: La Piscine is an incubator dedicated to social economy start-ups. It offers specific support for projects with a social impact.

> **These incubators have contributed to the success of many start-ups by providing resources, quality mentoring and opportunities for growth. They represent different business sectors and geographical areas, offering entrepreneurs a wide range of options for bringing their ideas to fruition.**

- **Mentors : Guides on your path**

A mentor is your entrepreneurial compass. These experienced guides have already traveled the paths you're exploring. Their role is to give sound advice, share their experience and help you avoid obstacles. A mentor is like a lighthouse that lights your way through the sometimes tumultuous waters of entrepreneurship.

- **Organizations for young entrepreneurs**

Joining an organization dedicated to young entrepreneurs is like joining a brotherhood of adventurers. You're part of a like-minded community, with events, workshops and networking opportunities. These organizations offer a solid network where young people can exchange ideas, find partners and grow together. It's like having a family that celebrates your victories and supports you in your difficulties.

- **Recommended equipment**

Eternal notebook: Record all ideas, thoughts and lessons learned. It's your personal guide to the world of entrepreneurship.

Vision Compass: Always keep a clear vision. This is the compass that guides you when the going gets tough.

Perseverance sword: Perseverance is the sword that gives you the strength to persevere in the face of obstacles. Every entrepreneur needs a dose of steel to meet challenges.

Adaptability: always be ready to adapt. Like flexible armor, it protects you while enabling you to develop flexibly.

Networking: A gourd full of courage to help you approach new people and forge fruitful alliances.

> **Arm yourself well, young entrepreneur! These resources are here to guide you, inspire you and propel you towards new horizons. May your entrepreneurial adventure be grandiose, rich in discovery and crowned with success.**

Part 2

Essential entrepreneurial skills

In the vast entrepreneurial landscape, bold, visionary personalities emerge, equipped not only with ambitious dreams, but above all with the essential skills that propel them to success. The chapter we're about to launch looks at these core competencies that characterize successful entrepreneurs. Far beyond ideas and business models, this chapter explores the core competencies that forge an entrepreneur's trajectory, defining his or her ability to overcome challenges, make sound decisions and create successful businesses. Whether budding innovators or seasoned veterans, acquiring and honing these skills proves to be the pillars on which a sustainable entrepreneurial career rests. Get ready to plunge into the stimulating world of entrepreneurial skills, a territory where creativity, resilience and insight become the indispensable tools of success.

Creativity and innovation

Creativity and innovation are the keys to success for any entrepreneur, regardless of age or sector. If you want to create a company that stands out from the crowd, creativity will be your strength and innovation your secret weapon.

Creativity is the power to paint any masterpiece. It's thinking outside the box, exploring ideas that no one else has ever considered. For an entrepreneur, it's the ability to see opportunities where others see obstacles. Innovation is about turning creative ideas into something tangible and revolutionary.

Tips for unleashing creativity and cultivating innovation:

Cultivate curiosity: Ask questions. A lot of questions. Curiosity is the fuel of creativity. The more you know the more resources you have to create something extraordinary.

Curiosity encourages us to explore different fields and acquire diverse knowledge. It enables us to draw on multiple sources of inspiration, expand our intellectual horizons and create links between seemingly very different ideas. Curious minds are often problem-solvers. Curiosity encourages the exploration of different approaches and solutions, which in turn fosters creative problem-solving.

Curiosity encourages the creation of unexpected links between different concepts, industries or disciplines. These unexpected links are often the source of innovative and creative ideas. Breakthroughs and important innovations often occur when inquisitive minds challenge the status quo and come up with revolutionary ideas. Curiosity is at the root of innovation.

> Curiosity is the fuel of creativity, nourishing the thirst for knowledge, stimulating original thinking and encouraging exploration. Creative entrepreneurs see curiosity as a powerful engine for discovering new opportunities, solving complex problems and creating innovative, successful businesses.

Get out of your comfort zone: Creativity often lies at the frontier between the known and the unknown. Don't hesitate to think outside the box and take risks to explore new approaches. This is where the most innovative ideas are born.

When we step out of our comfort zone, our brains are exposed to new experiences and challenges. This stimulates brain activity, encourages creativity and the emergence of new ideas.

The comfort zone is often associated with routine and familiarity. Stepping outside this zone allows us to explore new ideas, see things in a new light and discover opportunities that might otherwise have gone unnoticed.

Fear of failure is a common obstacle to creativity. By stepping out of your comfort zone, you learn to accept failure as a normal part of the learning process. This frees the mind from the constraints associated with the fear of failure.

Stepping out of one's comfort zone fosters personal development by enabling the acquisition of new skills, strengthening resilience and broadening self-understanding. These elements are all essential to nurturing creativity, which often requires pushing conventional boundaries and exploring uncharted territory. Stepping out of one's comfort zone helps to overcome these limits and pave the way for innovative ideas and solutions.

> Creativity often flourishes when we take risks, explore unfamiliar territory and defy habit. Stepping out of your comfort zone unleashes your creative potential and provides a breeding ground for inspiration and innovation.

Think differently, act differently: Creativity isn't just about thinking differently, it's also about acting differently. It means being prepared to take risks and challenge the status quo.

Thinking differently means escaping traditional patterns of thought. It allows us to explore new perspectives, challenge established norms and find innovative solutions to problems. Creativity is often stimulated by a diversity of ideas. Thinking differently encourages the divergence of ideas by creating an environment conducive to the creation of multiple solutions and approaches.

Thinking differently opens the door to experimentation. People who adopt an innovative approach are often more willing to test new ideas, take calculated risks and learn from experience.

> Thinking and acting differently are the main catalysts of creativity, as they open the way to innovation, diversity of ideas and unique

Problems = Opportunities: See problems as hidden opportunities. Innovative entrepreneurs solve real problems. They identify challenges and create solutions that improve people's lives.

Seeing problems as opportunities involves a shift in mindset. It transforms a potentially daunting obstacle into a chance to find creative solutions and stimulate personal and professional growth.

Problems often present complex challenges that require creative thinking to solve. Seeing problems as opportunities stimulates creative thinking, encourages the generation of innovative ideas and the search for original solutions. Approaching difficulties from a creative point of view opens the way to new and innovative solutions that can lead to continuous improvement and competitive advantage. Instead of reacting passively to difficulties, it encourages initiative and anticipatory problem-solving.

The opportunities often hidden at the heart of problems can lead to the creation of value. Innovations born of creative problem-solving can not only overcome obstacles, but also generate new benefits and opportunities.

Listening to your audience: The best ideas for innovation often emanate from a clear understanding of the audience's needs. So it's imperative to listen, observe and adjust your ideas accordingly.

By listening to the audience, we can clearly identify the unmet needs and problems they face. Creativity is often triggered by the search for innovative solutions to these specific needs. Creative ideas can often be derived from audience comments, suggestions and feedback. By understanding what captivates or preoccupies the public, we can find innovative ways to bring value and engagement.

Public expectations evolve over time. Listening to your audience enables you to keep abreast of emerging trends and changes in behavior, fostering adaptability and creativity to respond to these evolutions and design solutions that really solve problems.

Audiences are often made up of people with different points of view. Listening to a plurality of voices broadens horizons and enables different perspectives to be considered, stimulating creativity by bringing in ideas from a variety of sources.

> Listening to the public helps us to design solutions that are relevant, innovative and in tune with real market needs. It's an essential way of keeping creativity grounded in reality, and creating products, services and experiences that resonate with the target audience.

Drawing inspiration from others (modeling): observe and learn from successful companies in your own and other sectors. Be curious and study current trends. This enables you to learn from the success of others and avoid their mistakes.

Drawing inspiration from others broadens horizons by exposing us to a variety of ideas, styles and perspectives. It nurtures creativity by introducing new influences and stimulating divergent thinking. By observing the work of others, we can discover new approaches, innovative techniques and original methods. This discovery can inspire new ways of thinking and approaching problems. Observing the creative work of others can act as a catalyst for creation. It can trigger associations of ideas, stimulate the imagination and inspire unique concepts.

Drawing inspiration from others allows us to learn by example. By studying the successes and failures of others, we can learn valuable lessons that fuel creative growth. It also fosters cooperation by creating an environment where ideas can be shared and improved collectively. Collaboration can lead to innovative solutions, thanks to the creative momentum it generates.

Drawing inspiration from others is an essential practice for unleashing creativity, as it enables us to explore, learn, adapt and innovate. It's a powerful way of enriching one's own creative process by drawing on the experiences and ideas of the wider creative community.

Time and priority management

Managing time and priorities is essential for every entrepreneur, whether a teenager or not. It's a key element in the success of any business.

Think of your time as a suitcase. You can't add to it, but you can decide what you put into it. Time management is about optimizing every moment to achieve your goals. Setting priorities means directing each instrument to create a harmonious melody.

Effective time management optimizes operational efficiency. Identifying and prioritizing essential tasks ensures efficient use of resources. Prioritization is crucial to aligning efforts with the company's strategic objectives. This ensures that all activities contribute significantly to achieving the company's long-term vision and objectives.

Poor time management can lead to organizational stress. Clearly defining priorities and allocating time efficiently creates a more balanced, less stressful working environment. This is essential for meeting commitments and deadlines, and for retaining the trust of customers, business partners and other stakeholders, thereby strengthening the company's reputation.

Time management improves productivity by focusing on the most important tasks and minimizing distractions. This fosters a work environment where teams can be more productive. When time management is valued within the company, it helps create a performance-oriented culture. Team members understand the importance of optimizing their time to make a significant contribution to the objectives set by the company.

Managing time and priorities is a fundamental skill for managers and teams in running a business. It contributes to operational efficiency, the achievement of strategic objectives and the creation of an environment conducive to innovation and growth.

Tips for managing your time like a pro:

Precise planning: The diary becomes your best friend. Plan your days carefully. A young entrepreneur juggling studies, business and leisure needs an electronic calendar, notebook, diary and reminders to stay on track.

Prioritize wisely: Everything is important, but not everything is urgent. Prioritize your tasks. Tackle the most crucial ones first. Someone launching a clothing line, for example, while still a student, prioritizes design, production and promotion. He prioritizes design, production and promotion, concentrating his energy where it counts most.

The magic of lists: Make lists. A concise to-do list can make the insurmountable manageable. Check off each item as you go along.

Divide and conquer: Break large projects down into smaller tasks. This makes them less daunting and allows you to progress step by step.

Saying "No" with delicacy: Learn to say no to things that don't contribute to your goals. It's hard, but it frees up time for what really matters. An entrepreneur who balances her time between her business and her passion for sport. She knows when to say no to opportunities that could upset her balance.

Avoid distractions: Avoid distractions like social media, online gaming and other non-productive activities. Focus on the tasks at hand and eliminate distractions as much as possible.

Letting your schedule breathe: Avoid overload. Leave room for the unexpected. This gives you the flexibility to deal with unexpected challenges. It's also important to take regular breaks to avoid exhaustion and stay motivated. Take a 5-10 minute break every hour to relax and recharge.

Setting limits: Everyone has hours of the day when they are most productive. Identify these times and plan your most important tasks during them. Establish clear boundaries between work and personal time. This helps to avoid burnout and maintain a good work-life balance.

Managing time and priorities isn't a chore; it's the key to success. So, young entrepreneur, plan smart, prioritize wisely and make your time dance.

Communication and negotiation skills

The acquisition of communication and negotiation skills is essential to the success of a business. A teenager who wants to become an entrepreneur needs to learn how to communicate effectively with customers, suppliers, business partners and employees. They also need to know how to negotiate contracts and agreements.

Consider each word as a precious stone. Communication is the art of assembling them to create an understandable jewel. For an entrepreneur, it's the key that opens every door. Negotiation is a dance where every gesture counts. Knowing how to negotiate means ensuring that all parties win.

Communication skills are essential for building strong interpersonal relationships. Positive relationships within the company foster a collaborative and supportive working environment. Leaders must clearly communicate their vision, goals and expectations. Strong communication skills are needed to inspire and motivate teams, facilitating effective leadership. Open and effective communication promotes collaborative decision-making. Team members can share their points of view and discuss options, resulting in better-informed and accepted decisions.

Conflicts can naturally arise in a professional environment. Negotiation and communication skills are needed to resolve these conflicts constructively and maintain a positive working climate.

Negotiation is an essential part of business operations. Negotiation skills are needed to reach advantageous agreements, whether with partners, customers or suppliers. Communication is also at the heart of marketing and sales. Negotiation skills are also useful for closing successful deals and building lasting relationships with customers. Transparent, honest communication is essential to managing a company's reputation. The way a company communicates influences external and internal perceptions of its credibility.

Tips for honing your communication and negotiation skills:

Active Listening: Be attentive to the other party's needs and concerns. When someone speaks, really listen. Ask questions to show you're interested in the conversation. This creates an atmosphere of mutual understanding.

Clarity and simplicity: be able to express yourself clearly and without hesitation. Avoid complicated jargon. Be clear and concise. The message must be understood by everyone, from the trainee to the general manager.

Positive body language: Our bodies speak too. Positive body language, with eye contact and an open posture, reinforces the impact of our words.

Empathy: be able to understand the emotions and feelings of other stakeholders.

Reactivity: be able to respond quickly and effectively to requests and questions.

Preparation: Before negotiating, you need to know your subject inside out. Anticipating questions and objections means being ready for anything by examining the objectives and priorities of each party.

Finding common ground: Be able to listen carefully to the other party to understand their needs and concerns. Look for win-win solutions. The best negotiation is one where everyone is satisfied with the outcome.

Persuasion and flexibility: be able to persuade of the value of the proposed offer and be ready to adapt to the needs and requirements of the other party.

Staying calm under pressure: Negotiations can be intense. Keeping your cool, even in tense moments, helps you strengthen your position.

- ✓ An entrepreneur speaks to a potential customer. He listens attentively, answers questions clearly and creates a bond that goes beyond business.
- ✓ A contractor negotiates the terms of a contract with a supplier. He knows what he wants, but he's also open to adjustments that benefit all parties.
- ✓ An entrepreneur who communicates effectively with his team. He inspires guides and ensures transparent communication to maintain a positive work atmosphere.

> Communication and negotiation are the pillars of a successful business. So speak eloquently, listen carefully and negotiate finely. These skills will propel you to the heights of entrepreneurship.

Managing income and expenses

Managing income and expenses is an essential part of being an entrepreneur. It's important to understand how to effectively manage your company's cash flow to ensure its long-term growth and viability.

Think of revenue as the good rain and expenses as the fertile soil. For your business to thrive, you need to find the perfect balance between these two forces.

Effective management of revenues and expenses contributes to the company's financial stability. It helps maintain a balance between revenues and costs, ensuring the company's long-term viability. A thorough understanding of revenues and expenses provides a solid basis for informed decision-making. Managers can assess the profitability of various projects, investments and initiatives, facilitating informed strategic decision-making.

Managing revenues and expenses is at the heart of budget planning. By understanding projected cash flows and associated costs, the company can develop realistic, achievable budgets. Preventive revenue and expense management helps reduce financial risks. It involves constant monitoring of trends, early identification of potential financial problems and implementation of corrective measures.

Comparing revenues and expenses enables us to assess the profitability of the company as a whole, or of specific sectors. It helps to direct efforts towards the most profitable activities, and to identify areas requiring adjustment. It enables savings to be made. By optimizing operating costs, the company can maximize its profit margins and strengthen its competitiveness in the marketplace.

Transparent management of revenues and expenses helps build trust with stakeholders, including investors, customers and employees. Financial transparency is essential to building strong relationships with these parties. It also ensures compliance with legal and tax obligations. This avoids financial penalties and preserves the company's reputation.

Strategies for managing your finances:

The budget: The first step towards effective management of company finances is to draw up a clear, detailed budget. The budget will enable you to plan expenses, forecast income and determine the amount of money that can be invested in developing the business. Draw up a realistic budget. List all possible revenues and forecast future expenses. This gives you a clear picture of your financial situation.

Accounting: Accurate accounting is essential for managing a company's finances. It involves keeping complete records of financial transactions, including invoices, receipts, payments and tax returns.

Anticipation: Income can fluctuate. So you need to anticipate the ups and downs by creating reserves for calmer periods.

Smart investments: Les entrepreneurs doivent connaître les différents types d'investissement disponibles pour les petites entreprises. Il est essentiel de comprendre les risques et les avantages de chaque option d'investissement avant de prendre une décision. Chaque dépense doit contribuer à la croissance de l'entreprise et être investie judicieusement dans des domaines qui auront un impact positif.

Invoice management: A contractor must be able to invoice customers correctly and keep track of payments to avoid late payments and uncollectible debts. Send invoices promptly and follow up payments rigorously. This helps maintain a steady flow of income.

Tax management: Entrepreneurs need to know what their company's tax obligations are, and how to minimize or optimize them. The advice of an accountant or tax specialist can prove invaluable in tax planning. Set aside a portion of income for tax purposes, so that when the time comes, the company can pay it.

Eliminate unnecessary expenses: A contractor needs to be vigilant about how he spends his money, and seek to minimize unnecessary costs. Expenses need to be monitored regularly to ensure that the company stays within budget. Review all expenses. Eliminate those that don't add value. Every euro counts.

Use of financial management tools: There are many financial management tools, such as accounting software and cash management applications, which can help entrepreneurs, manage their finances effectively.

QuickBooks: This popular accounting software simplifies financial management, from billing to bookkeeping.

Wave: Wave offers accounting and invoicing functions, and is particularly popular with small businesses.

FreshBooks: It's online invoicing and accounting software designed for the self-employed and small businesses.

Xero: Xero is an online accounting platform offering invoicing, bank accounting and project management functionalities.

Zoho Books: This application offers online accounting, invoicing and expense management functions.

Expensify: This is an excellent tool for managing expense reports. It allows you to track business expenses and generate reports.

Mint: Although more focused on personal financial management, Mint can also be useful for tracking business expenses.

Sage: It offers accounting and financial management solutions for companies of all sizes.

QuickFile: Free online accounting software with basic functionality for small businesses.

> Managing revenues and expenses isn't just a matter of numbers on a sheet of paper. It's the financial synergy that keeps your business on the road to success. It's possible to plan, anticipate and invest wisely.

Part 3

Company management

Business management is a complex and dynamic art, skilfully combining strategy, operational planning and tactical decision-making. This chapter looks at the nuts and bolts of running a business, exploring the many facets required to ensure its viability, growth and longevity. From financial management to team leadership to strategic goal setting, we examine the crucial skills that every leader and manager must master to run a successful business. In this journey through the challenges and opportunities of business management, we'll discover how an enlightened approach can not only overcome obstacles, but also foster innovation, boost performance and build a solid foundation for the future.

Employee and partner management

Managing employees and partners is an important step in business development. Whether we're a sole trader or a start-up, we may one day need to hire employees or collaborate with partners to achieve our business goals.

Effective employee management promotes productivity by creating a positive work environment. Well-managed teams are generally more committed, motivated and efficient. Attentive management contributes to talent retention. Employees who feel valued and supported in their professional development are more likely to stay with the company.

Employee management influences the work climate. A positive corporate culture, created by attentive management, fosters collaboration, creativity and employee well-being. It encourages the acquisition of new skills, capacity building and career advancement, benefiting both the individual and the company.

Managing business partners is just as essential. Establishing and maintaining strong relationships with partners strengthens the supply chain, fosters trust and can lead to fruitful business opportunities.

Well-informed employees and strong partnerships enable the company to respond effectively to changing market needs. This provides a competitive advantage by fostering organizational agility, and directly influences team dynamics, corporate culture, capacity for innovation and the way the company is perceived, both internally and externally.

Creating a winning team :

Recruit wisely: Like the coach of a soccer team, you need to choose players who complement your skills. The balance between strengths and weaknesses creates an unbeatable team. If the company is growing and needs to hire additional staff, it may be necessary to consider setting up a human resources department. This department will be responsible for employee management, payroll and personnel administration.

Inspiration and motivation: Be the inspiring captain of your team. Motivation and enthusiasm are contagious. If you believe in your vision, they will too. Motivating your employees or partners is important for maintaining their commitment to the company. You can motivate them by offering benefits, bonuses, training or opportunities for advancement.

Promoting communication: Like a conductor, encourage open communication. Everyone needs to understand their role to create a harmonious symphony. To this end, it's a good idea to hold regular meetings to discuss the company's progress, challenges and next steps.

Choosing your travel companions: Partners are like teammates on a common quest. They must be chosen wisely, as their commitment and skills will have a direct influence on the company's success. It's important to define the roles and responsibilities of each employee or partner to avoid misunderstandings and conflicts by ensuring that everyone involved understands their role and contribution to the business.

Solid contracts: Draw up clear, solid contracts. A successful partnership is built on a stable legal foundation. Think of it as the golden rule of business.

Cultivating a win-win relationship: A successful partnership is a dance in which each partner plays an important role. Care must be taken to ensure that the benefits are mutual and that there is something in it for everyone.

Conflict management: Conflicts can arise within a team. Appropriate management helps to resolve these conflicts constructively, thus fostering a harmonious and productive environment.

Like a skilled diplomat, he resolves conflicts with elegance. Open communication and the search for solutions are the keys to overcoming obstacles. Conflicts can arise in any business. It's important to resolve them quickly and effectively to prevent them from disrupting the business. Conflict management protocols need to be put in place, and the presence of a mediator should be considered in the event of persistent conflict.

Constructive feedback: Be ready to receive and give feedback. It's a powerful tool for continuous improvement, like tuning the chords of a melody.

Adapting to change: The business world is an ever-changing symphony. You have to be ready to adjust your score according to the needs of the moment. Well-managed teams are better able to adapt to organizational change. Transparent communication and resistance management contribute to a smooth transition.

Strategic planning and decision-making

Strategic planning and decision-making are very important for any entrepreneur, whether novice or experienced. In this chapter, we dive into the deep waters of intelligent planning and informed decision-making.

Strategic planning establishes the company's long-term direction and vision. It defines fundamental objectives and guides decision-making towards the realization of these aspirations. It enables optimal allocation of resources, including time, money and talent. It helps determine priorities and focus efforts on the most important initiatives.

Good strategic planning enables a company to adapt to changes in the market, technology and business environment. It fosters flexibility and the ability to seize new opportunities while minimizing risks. It provides a clear understanding of competitive advantages and areas for improvement.

The objectives defined as part of the strategic planning process serve as a benchmark against which to measure the company's performance. This makes it possible to measure progress, identify necessary adjustments and optimize results. By anticipating market trends and developing adaptive strategies, strategic planning contributes to the long-term viability of the company, enabling it to remain relevant and successful over time.

The Art of Strategic Planning:

Define your vision: Like an explorer mapping an unknown land, start by clearly defining your vision. Where do you want your company to be in five or ten years? This vision will be your compass.

Analyze the terrain: Like a military strategist assessing the battlefield, it's an evaluation of external trends and factors that may affect the business, such as market trends, competition, opportunities and government regulations. This in-depth understanding will guide your strategy.

Setting SMART objectives: This involves defining the company's long-term objectives based on the results of the environmental analysis and the identification of strengths and weaknesses. Like an athlete setting training goals, establish SMART (Specific, Measurable, Attainable, Realistic, Time-bound) objectives. These goals are the milestones on your journey.

Gathering crucial information: it involves gathering all relevant information to evaluate the options available. Like detective gathering clues, collect all relevant information. Informed decisions are the foundation of a successful business.

Weighting options: This involves evaluating each option in terms of its advantages and disadvantages, as well as its potential impact on the business. Like a chess player evaluating every possible move, weigh up the pros and cons of each option. The best decision is often the one that best aligns with your vision.

Consult your team: Like a political leader gathering his cabinet, consult your team. Different perspectives can illuminate angles you might not have thought of.

Decision-making: This involves choosing the best option based on the results of the options analysis, and putting in place an action plan to implement the chosen decision.

Contractor's tools :

SWOT matrix: Think of the SWOT matrix as a star map, showing you strengths, weaknesses, opportunities and threats. It's your guide to strategy.

1. Identification of Strengths :

Identify the internal aspects of your company that are assets. These may include qualified human resources, specific skills, tangible assets such as technology or equipment, and competitive advantages.

Examples: talented team, cutting-edge technology, strong brand reputation.

2. Identifying Weaknesses:

Identify internal aspects that represent challenges or weaknesses. This may include skill gaps, inefficient processes, limited resources or other aspects that could hamper performance.

Examples: Lack of staff training, inefficient production processes, over-reliance on a single customer.

3. Identifying Opportunities :

Identify market trends, technological developments, regulatory changes or other external factors that could create opportunities for your company.

Examples: New emerging markets, technological advances, and favorable legislative changes.

4. Identifying Threats :

Identify external factors that could represent risks or threats to your business. This could include increased competition, economic changes, adverse technological developments, etc.

Examples: Intense competition, exchange rate fluctuations, changing consumer preferences.

5. Building the SWOT Matrix :

Draw a four-quadrant table with the sections "Strengths", "Weaknesses", "Opportunities" and "Threats". Places the Identified Elements: Place each identified element in the corresponding section of the table. This visually creates the SWOT matrix.

6. Relationship analysis :

Analyze the relationships between the different sections of the matrix. How can you use your strengths to seize opportunities? How can you mitigate weaknesses that could be exploited as threats?

7. Strategy Development :

Based on your analysis, develop strategies that capitalize on strengths, mitigate weaknesses, exploit opportunities and mitigate threats.

Examples: exploit key expertise, improve internal weaknesses, and diversify offerings to seize new opportunities, implement contingency plans to deal with threats.

> The SWOT matrix is not static. Revise it periodically to reflect changes in your company and its environment.

Decision tree: The decision tree is like a mind map, a visual process that allows you to represent the choices and consequences associated with each decision, helping you to visualize each option and its ramifications. It's a powerful tool for choosing the best path.

The goal

/ \

Decision A   Decision B

/ \   / \

Option 1 Option 2 Option 3

▼   ▼   ▼

Conseq.1 Conseq.2 Conseq.3

Clearly identify the purpose of the decision. It could be to solve a problem, to choose between different options, or to evaluate the potential results of a decision. Draw up a list of the main decisions that need to be made to achieve the objective. These are the points of divergence in your decision tree. For each main decision, list the different options available. These are the branches of the tree. For each option, identify the possible consequences, both positive and negative. These are the leaves of the tree, representing the outcomes or impacts associated with each choice.

For each consequence, we need to assess the probabilities associated with each outcome. This quantifies the risks and benefits of each option. Once the decision tree has been created, analyze the various options and their consequences. Based on preferences, objectives and acceptable risks make the decision that seems most appropriate.

Every decision you make and every plan you develop is a step forward.
May this exploration of strategic planning and decision-making guide
you towards prosperous and fulfilling horizons!

Business performance assessment and risk management

Risk management and business performance evaluation are essential elements of any successful entrepreneurial strategy. In this section, we'll take a closer look at these two key concepts, and discuss the strategies and tools needed to implement them in business.

Performance evaluation is used to determine the extent to which a company is achieving its strategic and operational objectives. This includes sales performance, profitability, customer satisfaction, etc. Performance analysis enables the company to identify strengths to be reinforced and weaknesses to be improved. In this way, it focuses its efforts on those areas which have the greatest impact on overall success.

By assessing performance, the company ensures continuous alignment with its objectives. This ensures that day-to-day actions contribute to the achievement of long-term aspirations.

Risk management identifies and assesses potential threats that could adversely affect the company. This includes financial, operational, strategic and other risks. Once risks have been identified, risk management involves planning mitigation actions. This involves implementing strategies to minimize the negative effects or maximize the opportunities associated with these risks.

In many sectors, risk management is crucial to ensuring compliance with regulations and standards. Anticipating and managing these risks helps to avoid the company incurring penalties and preserves its reputation. The trust of customers, partners and investors depends on the company's ability to manage risks responsibly.

Performance evaluation:

Define key performance indicators (KPIs): Like a pilot following his instruments, define your KPIs. These indicators show you the overall health of your business, whether in terms of sales, customer satisfaction or operational efficiency.

Key performance indicators are quantifiable measures of business performance, used to track and measure company results in key areas such as revenue growth, profitability, customer satisfaction, employee productivity, etc.

- **Dashboards:** Dashboards are visual tools used to monitor company KPIs.
- **Customer surveys:** Customer surveys provide feedback on the company's products and services, and identify areas for improvement.
- **Market research:** Market research enables us to gather data on market trends and consumer behavior, so that we can adapt our strategy accordingly.
- **Identify potential risks:** Like a captain anticipating storms, identify potential risks. This could include market changes, quality problems, or even external situations such as a pandemic.
- **Financial risks**: Financial risks relate to cash flow, investments and costs.
- **Operational risks:** Operational risks relate to internal processes, product and service quality, and regulatory compliance.

- **External risks:** External risks are linked to external factors such as market changes, political shifts, natural disasters, etc.

Risk management strategies

Like a strategist assessing the scope of an attack, evaluate the potential impact and probability of each risk. This allows you to prioritize and focus on the most critical ones. Develop preventive action plans. These plans are like lifelines in case of difficulties.

- **Diversification:** Diversification involves spreading risk over several products, services or markets to minimize the impact of a single risk.
- **Insurance:** Insurance is a strategy for transferring risk to a third party.
- **Business continuity planning:** Business continuity planning enables a company to prepare for emergencies and reduce business disruption in the event of a disaster.

Analysis and adjustment: Like an athlete scrutinizing his training statistics, regularly analyze the results. This allows you to identify areas of success to celebrate and areas of improvement to address, and adapt your trajectory according to the results. If something is working well, amplify it. If something isn't, adjust it.

> Navigating the waters of entrepreneurship can be tumultuous, but with constant evaluation and astute risk management, you'll be ready to weather every storm and sail toward prosperous horizons!

Part 4

Practical advice on how to succeed as a teenage entrepreneur

Find mentors and support networks

Mentors and support networks can provide valuable guidance, advice and resources to help young entrepreneurs achieve their goals.

A mentor is an experienced and competent person who offers guidance, advice and support to a less experienced person, often referred to as the mentee. The mentor shares his or her knowledge, experience and skills to help the mentee achieve professional or personal goals. The mentoring relationship can take many forms, from informal advice to structured programs.

A support network is a group of people who offer support, assistance and resources to an individual. This network can include colleagues, friends, family members, mentors and others who share common interests or goals. A support network can provide advice, perspectives, professional opportunities, as well as emotional and psychological encouragement.

Once the young entrepreneur has identified a potential mentor, it's important to understand how to build a solid relationship with him or her. This can include strategies such as prior research, setting clear objectives and maintaining the relationship on a regular basis.

The Importance of Mentors: Guides in the dark

Experience transmitted: Mentors are like lanterns lighting the rocky path of entrepreneurship. Their past experiences become a source of inspiration and practical lessons.

Personalized advice: Imagine you had a specific GPS for your entrepreneurial journey. Mentors provide advice tailored to your unique situation and help you avoid common mistakes.

Networking made easy: Mentors can open doors through their own networks. It's like having a VIP pass to key industry events.

Strategies for finding mentors :

Local and industrial events: Participate in local and industry events. Mentors are often present, ready to share their expertise.

Online platforms: Explore online platforms dedicated to connecting mentors and mentees. It's like a marketplace where you can find the perfect mentor.

Expand your network: Diversity is where the magic happens. Expand your network beyond your usual sphere to meet mentors from a variety of backgrounds.

Sharing experiences: Joining a support network connects you with other entrepreneurs sharing similar experiences. It's like a community of adventurers sharing their maps and tips.

Access to resources: These networks are like living libraries. You'll find resources, tools and practical advice that others have tried and tested.

Motivation and emotional support: Entrepreneurship is also an emotional journey. Support networks offer a shoulder to lean on and encouragement when the winds are unfavorable.

Finding mentors and support networks is like putting together a team of superheroes for your entrepreneurial adventure. With these allies at your side, you're ready to conquer the world of business!

Balancing entrepreneurship with studies and other activities and commitments

Entrepreneurship can be an exciting and rewarding activity for teenagers, but that doesn't mean they have to sacrifice their school life or other important activities. Balancing entrepreneurship with other commitments can be difficult, but it's an important skill for success in both areas.

You have your entrepreneurial passion on one side and a myriad of commitments on the other. How do you keep all those balloons in the air without dropping a single one? That's exactly what we're going to explore in this chapter.

Balance as the key to success

Entrepreneurship shouldn't overshadow the rest of your life. It's more like an important piece of a larger puzzle. Finding balance is the key to excelling in all areas of your life. Entrepreneurship is super important, but it doesn't have to eat everything up, because you've got other important pieces to fit in. The idea is not to let your business obscure everything else. Yeah, you want to succeed in entrepreneurship, but you also have your social life, your family, your hobbies, all that.

Because if you put everything into your job and neglect the rest, it's like trying to solve the puzzle with just one piece. You need every piece to make the picture complete.

So balance isn't a guru thing, it's a reality. It doesn't mean you have to sacrifice your professional success for the rest, but rather that you can excel everywhere if you have the right combination. Basically, take care of your business, but also take the time to spend with your friends, enjoy your family and do what you're passionate about. That's what's going to make your life truly successful.

Studies as allies:

Your studies are not in competition with your business, they are its allies. Use the skills you acquire at school to strengthen the foundations of your business.

So forget the "I don't have time for school, I'm too busy with my biz" nonsense. No, your studies aren't an obstacle; they're your secret weapon. Everything you learn, you can throw into the battle of your business. Courses are like a training room for you and your business. It strengthens the foundations.

And, let's be honest, when you show up with diplomas, it gives your credibility a serious boost. Customers and partners see that you're not there to mess around, you're there to rock.

Efficient prioritization :

You're like the conductor of your own circus. Learn to prioritize. Some commitments require more attention at certain times.

Energy reserves:

Entrepreneurship can be energy-consuming, but it's also a source of energy. Make sure you keep a reservoir of energy to keep everything moving.

Running a business can be exhausting, but it's also energizing. You just have to make sure you've always got enough energy to keep things running smoothly.

Entrepreneurship is like a machine that's running at full throttle and needs constant fuel to stay in the race. Every choice, every project pumps energy, and it never stops.

Don't forget that energy in entrepreneurship isn't just physical. It's also in your head, in your emotions. It's a balance you have to strike if you want to stay on top of your game.

To ensure the survival of his business, the entrepreneur needs to recharge his batteries regularly. Breaks, leisure activities and moments of relaxation are beneficial and help to gain perspective.

By keeping energy reserves in stock, the entrepreneur gives himself the means to overcome setbacks, innovate and see far ahead. Energy management is not just a question of immediate productivity; it's also a means of securing the long-term future of the company.

In short, just as a car needs a full tank of gas, the entrepreneur needs to keep his energy topped up to keep his company moving forward. Investing in this means ensuring a resilient business that grows over time in this fast-paced world of entrepreneurship.

Managing stress like a pro:

When stress becomes part of your daily routine, you need to be able to handle it like a boss. Life is a bit like juggling many things, and sometimes stress creeps in without warning. But rather than panic, you need to develop your own anti-stress weapons. This could be meditation, to clear your head, or letting off steam through sport, or even taking a relaxing break.

It's important to find out what works for you, because what works for one person may not work for another. It's a bit like having your own anti-stress magic wand that follows you everywhere. Whether its meditation, sport or a simple moment of relaxation, you need to find the answer that suits you. That way, even when everything seems out of whack, you can keep your professional composure.

Learning to say no :

It's like a delicate caper. You have to learn to say no to commitments that may overload your schedule, and yes to those that are in line with your goals. Sometimes we find ourselves saying yes to everything, even when we're already giving it our all.

Saying no isn't just about saying no. It's saying yes to yourself, to your goals, to your well-being. It's not about saying no to things, it's about choosing what makes you tick.

Avoid common mistakes made by young entrepreneurs

Becoming an entrepreneur at a young age can be exciting, but it can also bring unique challenges. Here are a few tips to help you avoid common mistakes and succeed in your mission.

Underestimating planning: Proper planning is essential to the success of any business. Young entrepreneurs may be tempted to skip the planning stages because of their enthusiasm and impatience. However, careful planning can help prevent unnecessary problems and risks. Take the time to create a detailed plan. Where do you want to go? How do you plan to get there? What are the possible obstacles? A good quest map will guide you through the difficult terrain.

Underestimating costs: Young entrepreneurs tend to underestimate the costs associated with setting up and running a business. It's important to conduct thorough research to understand all the costs associated with your business, including hidden costs such as licenses and permits.

Ignoring feedback: Great minds learn from others. Don't make the mistake of thinking you can do it all yourself. Mentors, experienced entrepreneurs and even your peers can be a goldmine of advice. Don't be afraid to ask for advice and learn from the experiences of others. Don't be afraid to ask for advice and learn from the experiences of others. However, it's important to understand that criticism can help improve your business and make it grow. Be open-minded and ready to receive constructive feedback.

Neglecting the power of perseverance: Rome wasn't built in a day, and neither is your quest. Setbacks and failures are part of the journey. You mustn't give up at the slightest difficulty. Every trial is an opportunity to learn and grow stronger. Bear in mind that the most legendary heroes have overcome countless challenges before succeeding.

Forgetting the importance of flexibility: The best map in the world can't predict every twist and turn of a quest. Be prepared to adjust your plan along the way. Flexibility is a powerful weapon. If a monster appears in your path, you may be forced to change course. Be agile and adaptable.

Neglecting balance in your life: Even the greatest heroes need a rest. Don't let your quest overwhelm you to the point of sacrificing your well-being. Balancing your entrepreneurial life, your studies and your hobbies is the key to a fulfilled hero.

Do not delegate: Young entrepreneurs may find it difficult to delegate tasks to other team members. However, it's important to delegate to enable the business to grow and develop. You need to hire people you can trust to help you with your business, and delegate tasks that don't require your immediate attention.

Not being patient: Young entrepreneurs may have unrealistic expectations of growth and success. However, it's important to understand that growing a business takes time. Be patient and focus on building a solid, sustainable business.

- ✓ Thoroughly research and develop a solid business plan.
- ✓ Carefully evaluate all the costs associated with your business.
- ✓ Be open to constructive feedback and use it to improve your business.
- ✓ Hire people you trust to help you, and delegate tasks that don't require your immediate attention.
- ✓ Be patient and focus on building a solid, sustainable business.

- ✓ Books on entrepreneurship: There are plenty of books on entrepreneurship dealing with common mistakes to avoid.
- ✓ Case studies: Case studies are an excellent resource for understanding the mistakes made by other entrepreneurs and the lessons they learned from those mistakes. There are several websites that offer case studies on entrepreneurship, such as Harvard Business Review, Entrepreneur, Forbes and Inc.
- ✓ Mentors and coaches: Mentors and coaches can offer personalized advice and guidance on how to avoid common entrepreneurial mistakes. They can share their own experience and provide practical advice on how to avoid the mistakes they have made.
- ✓ Discussion groups and social networks: Online discussion groups and social networks can provide a forum for asking questions and discussing the challenges of entrepreneurship with other entrepreneurs. LinkedIn groups, Reddit forums, Facebook groups and communities on Slack are all good places to find discussions about entrepreneurship.
- ✓ Entrepreneurship events: Entrepreneurship events such as conferences, workshops and seminars can offer opportunities to learn from experts and experienced entrepreneurs. Events such as TEDx, SXSW and Startup Weekend are all good examples of entrepreneurship events to consider.
- ✓ Business gas pedals: Business gas pedals offer a range of services to help entrepreneurs develop their businesses, including personalized advice, training sessions and networking opportunities. Gas pedal programs such as Y Combinator, Techstars and Seedcamp are all good examples to consider.

By avoiding these common pitfalls, you'll be more likely to succeed in your entrepreneurial quest. Remember, you're the hero of your story, so get ready to take on the challenges and conquer the heights.

From idea to reality: Turning a concept into a thriving business

If you have to summarize everything you've learned in this book to make your idea a reality, here are the main steps in the business creation process, followed by 10 practical exercises designed to develop your entrepreneurial skills:

So you're armed with an idea that makes your heart beat faster and ignites your entrepreneurial spirit. Great stuff! The crucial question now is: how do you take this idea from dream to reality? Here are a few key steps that will help you turn your concept into a thriving business.

1. Validating your idea :

Start by making sure your idea is sound. Is there a real demand for what you're proposing? You need to study the market in depth, possibly interview your future users, and be ready to adjust your concept according to the feedback you receive.

The first question you need to answer is: is there a real demand for what you're proposing? Dive into the market you plan to conquer. You need to analyze current trends, unmet needs and identify the competition. Understanding your market will enable you to position your company so that it responds effectively to needs.

Your future users are the key to your success. Engage with them. Set up interviews, surveys or use other methods to get direct feedback. Ask open-ended questions that will help you understand their challenges, needs and expectations. Be open to constructive criticism, which is essential for refining your concept.

No idea is perfect from the start. Be prepared to adjust your concept according to the feedback you receive. If something doesn't work out as planned, don't consider it a failure, but rather an opportunity to learn and improve. Sometimes it's necessary to make a pivot, i.e. to change direction based on what you've learned from feedback. Be flexible and ready to adjust your initial plan to better meet market needs.

2. Draw up a business plan:

A business plan is like the map that guides your entrepreneurial journey. Detail your idea, your vision and how you plan to achieve your goals. Add financial projections to show that you've thought through the budgeting part. This plan will become your strategic guide.

Your business plan is the compass that will guide you through your entrepreneurial journey. More than just a document, it's a strategic roadmap that details every step of your journey to success.

First of all, explain your idea clearly. What is your vision? What makes your business unique? Explaining these elements in detail will give you a solid foundation on which to build. Clearly define your short- and long-term objectives. How do you intend to achieve them? What strategies will you use? A well-thought-out business plan aligns your actions with your ambitions.

Financial projections are the backbone of your business plan. It's important to detail initial costs and anticipated revenues, and to draw up a realistic budget. This is the proof that you've thought through the financial side of your business.

Identifies potential risks and develops strategies to mitigate them. A good entrepreneur doesn't ignore possible challenges, but prepares to overcome them with resilience.

Explain how you intend to implement your plan. What concrete steps will you take? Who will be involved? An operational roadmap turns ideas into concrete actions.

Your business plan becomes your strategic guide. Whether you're looking for investors, partners or simply to guide yourself, this comprehensive document is the reference that shows everyone that you have a clear vision and a well-thought-out strategy.

Drawing up a business plan may seem tedious, but it's an essential investment in your company's future. It shows your credibility as a serious entrepreneur and gives you a solid basis for making informed decisions at every stage of your journey.

3. Develops a prototype or minimum viable product (MVP):

Turn the abstract into the concrete, the idea into reality. If your project revolves around a physical product, creating a prototype or minimum viable product (MVP) is the next crucial step. Here's why and how this phase can propel your idea to success:

A prototype or MVP allows you to bring your idea to life. It's a tangible version of what you plan to create. It gives you the opportunity to test your concept in the marketplace.

The prototyping phase provides real feedback from potential users. It goes beyond assumptions and guesses. Real feedback will guide the evolution of your product. Feedback gives you the opportunity to adjust and improve your product. Perhaps there are aspects you hadn't considered, or features that could be improved. This phase is the ideal testing ground.

The creation of a prototype avoids the need to devote enormous resources to a full version of the product without having tested its market acceptance. This makes for more efficient management of financial and time resources.

If you're looking for investors, a solid MVP can be a formidable weapon. It shows that you've acted, that you've tested and that you're ready to evolve. Investors are more likely to back a project that has already taken this essential step.

When you show a prototype, you communicate your idea visually. This is often more convincing than simple descriptions. It can arouse the enthusiasm and interest of potential customers, partners or investors.

In short, creating a prototype is an essential and stimulating stage of the entrepreneurial journey. It's where your idea comes to life, where you begin to forge links with the real world, and where you lay the foundations for your company's future success. So go ahead, create, test and take your idea to new heights!

4. Financing :

Most businesses need some money to get off the ground. Whether you're saving, borrowing from family and friends or looking for investors, you need to explore different options for financing the business you want to set up.

Before soliciting outside investors, the first thing to think about is your own piggy bank. Saving wisely is an art that can provide the start-up capital you need. Analyze your expenses, draw up a realistic budget and save methodically. Every penny saved is a step closer to realizing your business idea.

Sometimes, the closest source can be the most beneficial. If family members or friends are willing to invest in the project, this option should be carefully considered. Clear, professional agreements are essential to avoid potential conflicts in the future.

Investors, whether venture capitalists or simply people with a passion for new ideas, can be the financial lifeline you need. It's important to prepare a solid presentation that highlights not only the financial aspect, but also the company's vision and growth potential.

Crowdfunding is a modern method of raising funds. Platforms such as Kickstarter or Ulule enable an idea to be presented to a wider public, who can decide to finance the project collectively. It's an innovative way of obtaining financial support from the general public.

Like government grants and loans for young entrepreneurs, many institutions provide financial support for entrepreneurial initiatives.

Participation in entrepreneurial competitions can not only bring funding, but also valuable exposure. Cash prizes, as well as industry recognition, can catalyze business start-ups.

Whether we're soliciting investors or asking for a loan, the key is preparation. You need to understand your financial needs, how you'll use the funds and how the business will generate revenue. The confidence you inspire can make all the difference.

Finding financing can be a complex but exciting journey. It's important to explore all possible options, prepare carefully and don't be afraid to share your vision with the world. Every penny raised is another step towards making your business projects a reality. So go for it with confidence, and may your ambitions be supported by the funding you need to turn your vision into reality.

5. Company registration :

You've taken some crucial steps, sculpted an idea into a concrete vision, and even secured the necessary funds. Now it's time to give your business a legal existence. Think of this step as the company's official birth certificate. Here's how to take your business from idea to legal reality.

The company name is more than just a label. It's the very essence of the company's identity. It should be chosen with care, ensuring that it is unique, memorable and in harmony with the company's value proposition. Also check that it complies with current legal regulations.

Registering a company involves some administrative formalities, but there's no need to worry. You need to find out about the specific requirements in your country and region. This may involve filing articles of association, declaring your business and obtaining a tax identification number. Some countries offer online one-stop-shops to facilitate these procedures.

Choosing the right legal structure for your business. Whether it's a sole proprietorship, a limited liability company (SARL) or a joint stock company (SA), each option has different tax, legal and liability implications. It's worth weighing up the pros and cons to find the one that best suits your entrepreneurial aspirations.

Registration procedures vary from place to place, but generally involve filling in specific forms, paying registration fees and providing documents such as the company's articles of association. It is advisable to consult the local authorities or to call on a professional to guide you through this administrative process.

If your company's business is based on unique products or services, intellectual property protection becomes crucial. Consider registering trademarks, patents or other intellectual property rights to protect the company's identity from competitors.

To keep personal and business finances separate, it is advisable to open a business bank account in the company's name. This simplifies financial management and strengthens the company's credibility in the eyes of customers and partners.

Examine insurance needs to protect the company against potential risks. This may include liability insurance, professional indemnity insurance or other types of insurance. It's an investment in your company's security.

Registering your business is much more than a formality. It's the step that gives it a legal existence and establishes the solid foundations on which it can grow. Choose carefully, fill in the paperwork accurately, and celebrate every step of the way, because this is where your dream officially becomes reality. Your vision now has a legal existence, and the world is ready to discover it.

6. Building your team :

No entrepreneur succeeds alone. Recruit people whose skills complement your own. A diverse team brings different perspectives and skills, strengthening the foundation of your business.

When building your team, look for people whose skills complement your own. If you're strong in a particular area, find teammates who excel where you may be lacking. It's the principle of complementarity that strengthens the whole.

A diverse team brings a variety of perspectives. People from different backgrounds see challenges and opportunities from unique angles. This diversity fosters creativity and innovation, crucial to staying competitive in the marketplace.

Each member of your team is like an essential brick in the construction of your company's edifice. The more solid and varied the bricks, the stronger the foundation. A well-built team strengthens the foundation, ensuring solid growth.

With a diversified team, the division of tasks can be managed more efficiently. Everyone can concentrate on what they do best, maximizing overall productivity. It also makes it possible to tackle a variety of challenges simultaneously.

A strong team is more than just a group of people working together. It's a cohesive whole, where collaboration is facilitated by a diversity of skills. A team that knows how to collaborate effectively overcomes obstacles with agility.

Working in a strong team also brings mutual support. Difficult moments are easier to overcome when you have teammates who share the same vision and are ready to support you. Motivation is mutually reinforcing, creating an environment conducive to fulfillment.

In conclusion, building a strong team is a vital investment in a company's success. Look for talented people. Together, they form a force capable of rising to challenges, exploiting opportunities and propelling the company to new successes. Recruiting wisely means building a team that will become the driving force behind your company's success.

7. Building your brand image :

Work on how you want others to perceive your company. Create a logo; choose colors and a font that represent the essence of your concept. The image of your brand must be memorable and correspond to our vision. Branding is the art of creating a memorable first impression and communicating the essence of what your company stands for. Here's how to bring your visual identity to life.

Before designing, we need to take the time to think about how people should feel when they think of our company. What emotion do we want to evoke? How do we want to be perceived? These answers will guide the process of creating our visual identity.

The logo is the company's eternal coat of arms. It must be simple, distinctive and represent the very essence of the company's activity. Whether it's an abstract symbol, stylized typography or a combination of the two, this logo will be the first thing people associate with the company.

Colors aren't just aesthetic; they have the power to communicate emotions. We need to opt for colors that reflect the atmosphere we want to create around our brand. Warm tones can inspire passion, while cool tones evoke confidence.

The font that accompanies the logo and communications has an impact on how people perceive a brand. An elegant font can suggest sophistication, while a more casual one can communicate a sense of accessibility.

Once the visual elements have been defined, it's important to use them consistently. This creates instant recognition. Whether on the website, on business cards or on social networks, visual consistency must always be maintained to reinforce the brand image.

A company's brand image is not set in stone. As the company evolves, certain elements may need to be adjusted. Don't hesitate to test different variations and gather feedback to continually refine your brand image.

Every company has a story. It's important to integrate elements of our history, values and mission into our branding strategy. This allows potential customers to make an emotional connection with what the company offers.

Originality is key. Don't just copy what works for others. Be authentic, because that's what will make the company memorable. The best brands are those that remain true to their unique identity.

Building a brand image is an opportunity to create a visual and emotional bond with your audience. It's essential to take the time to get it right, because a strong brand image can be the element that sets a company apart from its competitors and makes it unforgettable. The way you present yourself visually is the first impression people will have of your company, so make sure it's something extraordinary.

8. Launching

You've sculpted your idea, charted your course with a solid business plan, built a dynamic team, and created a brand image that exudes the essence of your vision. Now it's time to take flight, to unleash your company into the competitive arena of the business world. Here's how you can turn all that hard work into a successful launch.

It all starts with the first step. Don't feel the pressure to conquer the world right from the start. Start small, test your concept in a controlled environment, and adjust your strategy according to the feedback.

Learning never stops. Every day is a new lesson in the book of your entrepreneurship. Be open to new experiences, learn from mistakes and successes, and use this knowledge to continually refine your strategy.

The market is your best teacher. Listen carefully to what it tells you. Customer feedback, market trends and competitive movements are all clues that can guide you in the evolution of your business.

Flexibility is the key to success. If you encounter unexpected obstacles or opportunities, be ready to adjust your course. Sometimes the final destination remains the same, but the road to get there can take unexpected turns.

Every step you take is a victory. Whether it's the first sale, the launch of a product, or securing a partnership, take the time to celebrate these small victories. They're the gems that build the road to success.

Relationships are the currency of business. Build strong relationships with your customers, your partners, even your competitors. An engaged community around your business can be one of your greatest assets.

Entrepreneurship is a marathon, not a sprint. To stay committed over the long haul, maintain the passion that drove you to create your business. Getting up every day with the enthusiasm to make a difference is a powerful force.

There will be ups and downs. Realistic optimism is the mindset that will get you through the tough times while keeping you focused on the opportunities ahead.

> Launching your business is like sending a message in a bottle to the sea. You never know where it might end up, but you know you've created something precious. So launch yourself with confidence, determination and the certainty that you have what it takes to succeed in this exciting entrepreneurial adventure.

Practical exercises

Exercise 1 : Identifie problems, proposes solutions

Explore your community in search of challenges. Identify a problem that challenges you and propose an innovative solution. Whether it's an application, a service or an idea, this exercise will develop your ability to solve concrete problems.

The aim of this exercise is to sharpen your sense of observation and creativity by identifying real problems in your community and proposing innovative solutions. Following these steps will guide you through the process:

- Take the time to look closely at your community, whether it's your school, your neighborhood or even broader issues.
- Identify a problem that seems significant to you and that could benefit from a solution.
- Analyze the problem you've identified in depth. Understand its root causes, its impact on the community and why it needs a solution.
- Think of an innovative solution that could solve the problem effectively and sustainably.

Be creative! Think outside the box.

- Prepare a concise presentation of your solution. Use visual aids if necessary to make your proposal more striking.
- Be prepared to explain why your solution is unique and how it could be implemented.
- Share your proposal with friends, teachers and family. Get their opinions and suggestions.

- Be open to constructive criticism and ideas for improvement.
- Think about the potential impact of your solution on the community. How it could improve people's lives and solve the problem you've identified.

Exercise 2 : Entrepreneurial skills research

Conduct in-depth research into the skills you need to make this idea a success. Present your findings, highlighting the skills you already possess and those you wish to develop.

This exercise gives you the opportunity to delve into the skills needed to excel as an entrepreneur. These steps will help you better understand what's involved and identify your strengths and areas for development:

- Research essential entrepreneurial skills. These can include creativity, decision-making, problem-solving, communication, etc.
- Honestly assess your current skills. What skills do you already have? What are your strengths?
- Based on your research, identify the skills you'd like to develop. These could be related to time management, negotiation, financial management, etc.
- Organize your results in a structured presentation. Highlight key skills and briefly explain their importance.
- Based on the results, create a plan to develop the skills you want to strengthen. This could include attending workshops, reading books or even specific projects.
- Personal growth is an ongoing process. Continue to evaluate and adjust your plan as you progress along your entrepreneurial journey.

Exercise 3: SWOT analysis of your idea

Use a SWOT (strengths, weaknesses, opportunities, threats) analysis to evaluate your idea. Identify strengths to capitalize on, weaknesses to improve, opportunities to seize, and threats to anticipate.

SWOT analysis is a powerful tool for assessing the viability of your business idea. Here are a few steps to help you get an in-depth view of your business proposition:

- What are the strengths of your idea? These could be unique skills you possess, competitive advantages, specific experience, etc.
- What could be improved? This could include gaps in your skills, limited resources, potential obstacles, etc.
- What external opportunities could benefit your company? This could be related to market trends, unmet needs, potential partnerships, etc.
- What external obstacles and threats might you encounter? This could include competition, regulatory changes, financial risks, etc.
- Organize these factors in a SWOT matrix. This will help you clearly visualize the different aspects of your idea.
- Based on your SWOT analysis, develop strategies to capitalize on strengths, mitigate weaknesses, take advantage of opportunities and address threats.
- SWOT analysis can become an essential part of your business plan. Incorporate the findings into your strategic documentation.

Exercise 4: Creation of a simplified business plan

Develop a simplified business plan for your idea. Briefly describe the idea, vision, goals, marketing strategies, and financial projections. Here's how to do it:

- Briefly describe your business idea. What problem are you solving? What's your unique value proposition?
- State your company's long-term vision. What are your short- and long-term goals? Where do you see yourself in five years?
- What strategies will you use to promote your business? This could include online tactics, local partnerships, etc.
- Clearly define who your target audience is. Understand their needs, their behaviors and how your product or service meets those needs.
- Identify your main competitors. What differentiates you from them? How do you plan to stay competitive?
- How will your business generate revenue? This could include product sales, subscriptions, partnerships, etc.
- Develop simplified financial projections. This can include start-up costs, sales forecasts, monthly expenses, etc.
- Identify the main risks your company could face. What strategies do you have in place?
- Develop an action plan outlining the specific steps you'll take to launch and grow your business.
- Share your plan with friends, mentors and family. Get constructive feedback to refine your concept.
- Based on the feedback, adjust your business plan. Be ready to make changes to strengthen the viability of your business.
- Think of your business plan as a strategic guide. Consult it regularly and adjust it as your business evolves.

Exercise 5 : Virtual networking

Explore online professional networking platforms. Connect with entrepreneurs, ask them questions, and share your ideas. Virtual networking is a key skill in the modern business world. Here's how you can practice:

- Explore professional online platforms such as LinkedIn, Meetup, forums specialized in your field of activity or simply groups on social networks.
- If you don't already have one, create a professional profile. Make sure it reflects your background, your skills and, above all, your entrepreneurial project.
- Identify successful entrepreneurs in fields similar to yours. Follow them and explore their journeys.
- Take part in discussions by asking thoughtful questions. This could be related to specific challenges you're facing, or advice on running a start-up.
- Don't be shy about sharing your ideas. Open them up for discussion and solicit constructive feedback.
- Identify potential mentors. These are more experienced entrepreneurs who can offer you advice and guidance.
- Search for virtual events, webinars or online conferences related to entrepreneurship. Participate and expand your network.
- Join relevant groups on these platforms. Be active in discussions, share your expertise, and connect with other members.
- Virtual networking is not just about the quantity, but the quality of connections. Make genuine connections with people who share similar interests.
- If you identify entrepreneurs you admire, don't hesitate to ask them for an informal chat. Most are open to sharing their experiences.

- Always keep your tone professional. Even online, first impressions count.
- After a few weeks of activity, summarize your virtual networking experiences. What have you learned? Did you make any significant connections?

Exercise 6 : Building a virtual prototype

If your idea is digital, create a virtual prototype. Use online tools to simulate the user experience of your product or service. This will enable you to gather feedback before moving on to the development phase.

Here's how:

- Identify the essential features of your idea. What sets your product or service apart?
- Explore online tools for prototyping. Sketch, Figma, Adobe XD, and InVision are just a few examples. Choose the one that best suits your needs.
- Draw the main screens of your application or website. Focus on the user interface to give a visual idea of the experience.
- Use the tool's interactive features to simulate the navigation flow. This could include clickable buttons, links, etc.
- Test your prototype as if it were already a working application. This will give you an idea of the user experience and identify any usability problems.
- Share your prototype with friends, mentors, or even people in your community. Get feedback on visual appeal and ease of use.
- Use feedback to improve your prototype. Iteration is a crucial part of the development process.

- If your prototype simulates a complex product, document the technical specifications. This will help in the subsequent development stages.
- If your business model involves transactions, explore how this might work in your prototype. This could include sections for payments, subscriptions, etc.
- If you feel confident about your prototype, share it with other people interested in your project. This could include potential partners, investors or customers.
- Evaluate the technical viability of your prototype. Are the functionalities you envisage technically feasible?
- If you intend to present your idea to investors, prepare a visual presentation based on your prototype. This can include screenshots and interactive demonstrations.

Exercise 7 : Negotiation simulation

Imagine you're negotiating an agreement with a supplier or business partner. Simulate the negotiation, developing your communication and negotiation skills. Learn how to find win-win compromises.

- Choose a realistic negotiation scenario. It could be the purchase of raw materials, the conclusion of an agreement with a business partner, or any other situation relevant to your simulated company.
- Clearly define what you want to achieve through negotiation. What are your main objectives? This could include price conditions, delivery times, payment terms, etc.
- Anticipate areas where you're willing to compromise. Negotiation often involves finding common ground.
- Ask a friend, mentor or even colleague to play the role of supplier or business partner.

- Make sure this person is ready to play the game seriously.
- Prepare a clear and precise introduction. How will you present your points? How will you respond to counter-proposals? Be ready to adjust your communication according to the responses.
- Start the simulation as if it were a real negotiation meeting. Use professional language and stay focused on your objectives.
- If the discussion becomes tense, step back and try to understand the other party's perspective. Managing tension constructively is a key skill.
- Look for solutions that benefit both sides. A successful negotiation is not a competition, but collaboration.
- At the end of the simulation, conclude with a clear agreement. Summarize the agreed terms and make sure all parties are satisfied.
- After the simulation, analyze what went well and what could be improved. Also ask for feedback from the person who played the role of negotiating partner.
- Use the lessons learned from the simulation to readjust your negotiation strategy. It's a continuous learning process.

Exercise 8 : Practical financial management

Manage your company's finances virtually. Make projections, monitor income and expenses, and make informed financial decisions. It'll help you hone your financial management skills.

- Use tools such as Microsoft Excel, Google Sheets, or other spreadsheet software. Create sections for revenues, expenses, profits, losses, etc.
- Based on the information you have about your business (or a simulated business), make financial projections for

the coming months or years. Include expected sales, costs, taxes, etc.

- Introduce scenarios where you'll have to make decisions about potential investments. For example, consider buying equipment, launching a new product line, or investing in advertising.

- Regularly reviews financial data. Analyzes trends, identifies areas that are generating profits and those that may require adjustment.

- If you observe any financial problems or opportunities, readjust your financial strategy accordingly. Maybe you'll have to cut back on certain expenses, raise prices, or explore new sources of income.

- Include scenarios where you might need financing. Explore the different options, from self-financing to bank loans or finding investors.

- Cash flow is the lifeblood of any business. Learn how to manage cash flow, making sure you have enough cash to cover operating costs.

- Explore online financial management tools that can simplify this process. Some software is specifically designed to help entrepreneurs manage their finances.

- Introduce scenarios where unexpected events occur, such as a sudden drop in sales or an increase in costs. How would you adjust your financial strategy in the face of such challenges?

- Ask mentors, teachers or professionals to review your financial projections. External feedback can provide valuable insight.

Exercise 9 : The entrepreneurial pitch

Imagine you're standing in front of potential investors. Prepare a three-minute pitch to present your business idea. Be convincing, clear, and emphasize the unique aspects of your concept.

This exercise puts you in the shoes of an entrepreneur who has to present his idea to investors. Following these steps will help you develop your communication skills and refine the way you present your ideas:

- Clearly identify your company's core idea. What makes it unique and interesting?
- Divide your pitch into three parts: introduction, body and conclusion.

- In the introduction, capture attention with a punchy phrase.

- In the body, explain your idea in detail, emphasizing the benefits and opportunities.

- In the conclusion, summarize the key points and end on a strong note.

- Use clear, simple language. Avoid excessive jargon.
- Be convincing in your voice and posture. Self-confidence is crucial.
- Show your enthusiasm for your idea. Investors are attracted to passionate entrepreneurs.
- Create visual aids to accompany your pitch. This could be a PowerPoint presentation or simple graphics.
- Practice several times. The more familiar you are with your pitch, the more comfortable you'll feel during the actual presentation.

- Anticipate potential investor questions and prepare clear answers.
- Present your pitch to friends, teachers or mentors. Gather their feedback to improve your presentation.
- Be ready to adjust your pitch according to the feedback you receive. Adaptability is an essential entrepreneurial quality.

Register yourself (optional) :

If possible, record a video of your presentation. This will help you identify areas for improvement.

Exercise 10 : Post-launch analysis

Simulate the launch of your company and analyze the results. What feedback have you received from the market? What adjustments could you make? This exercise will help you develop the capacity for self-assessment and continuous adjustment.

- Imagine you've officially launched your business. Determine key variables such as sales, public reception, costs and returns.
- Simulate results using fictitious data. This can include sales figures, simulated customer feedback, and financial data based on your assumptions.
- Consider market feedback by recreating customer feedback, market analysis, and sales data. Analyzes trends, customer preferences, and competitive forces.
- Identify the aspects of your business that stand out and those that could use improvement. Also consider customer feedback and how you might better meet their needs.
- Examine the profitability of your business. Compare the initial costs with the revenues generated. If you've

invested money, evaluate the simulated return on investment (ROI).

- Based on your analysis, suggest potential adjustments. Perhaps you could improve the quality of a product, adjust your prices, or explore new marketing channels.
- Introduce alternative scenarios, such as sudden changes in the economy or the emergence of new competitors. How would your company react in these situations?
- Consider this simulation as a learning opportunity. What important lessons have you learned? How could you apply these lessons in a real-life context?
- If possible, share your simulated results with peers, mentors or teachers. External feedback can give you valuable insights.
- Finally, use these findings to plan your actual launch. What strategies will you draw from this simulation to ensure your company's success?

These practical exercises give you a hands-on opportunity to put the lessons in this book into practice. They are designed to develop your entrepreneurial skills and prepare you to face the challenges of the business world with confidence and creativity. Enjoy your work!

Some useful resources

Books

"The Minute Contractor" by Ken Blanchard and Don Hutson.

"Lean Startup" by Eric Ries.

"The $100 Startup" by Chris Guillebeau.

"Zero to One" by Peter Thiel.

Online Platforms

Coursera: Online courses on various topics related to entrepreneurship.

Udemy: Practical courses on starting up a business, marketing, etc.

LinkedIn Learning: Video courses on entrepreneurship and professional development.

Podcasts

"How I built this": Interviews with entrepreneurs who have built successful businesses.

"The Tim Ferriss Show": Conversations with successful personalities in a variety of fields.

Associations and Organizations

Junior Achievement: Encouraging young people to succeed in a global economy.

Enactus: A global community of students, teachers and business leaders committed to entrepreneurial action.

Events & Conferences

Participate in local or virtual events such as TEDx conferences, job fairs for young entrepreneurs, etc.

Mentoring

Look for a local or online mentor with experience in your field of interest.

Online Tools and Resources

Small Business Administration (SBA): Resources for entrepreneurs, including sample business plans.

SCORE: Free advice from mentors and online resources.

Blogs

Entrepreneur: Articles and advice on entrepreneurship.

Startup Grind: Resources for entrepreneurs and startups.

Conclusion

The advantages of becoming an entrepreneur at a young age

Entrepreneurship at a young age offers a myriad of benefits that go far beyond simply setting up a business. These benefits shape not only your career path, but also your personal development.

Starting a business is a hands-on education. It's an immersive experience where you discover tangible and intangible aspects of the business world. Every challenge is a lesson that contributes to your knowledge base. Entrepreneurship requires you to develop a variety of skills, from rapid decision-making to financial management and problem-solving. These skills, once acquired, stay with you for the rest of your life.

Young entrepreneurs often have a fresh and innovative perspective. It's a time when the creative spirit is at its peak, and this can lead to innovative and disruptive ideas.

Entrepreneurship teaches calculated risk-taking. This does not mean impulsivity, but rather a thoughtful assessment of risks and rewards. Learning to manage risk is an invaluable skill.

Being your own boss means having a certain degree of independence. It allows you to explore your own vision and make decisions without the limitations of a hierarchical structure. Entrepreneurship also gives you the opportunity to build a professional network at an early age. The relationships you build can prove invaluable throughout your career.

Starting a business at a young age means you have the flexibility to explore different ideas before settling on a specific path. This allows you to adjust and refine your goals as you grow.

Failure is an integral part of entrepreneurship. Learning to cope and bounce back from setbacks is a crucial skill that prepares you to overcome future obstacles.

Entrepreneurship at a young age is much more than starting a business. It's a journey of continuous learning, personal growth and self-discovery. The skills acquired and lessons learned lay the foundations for a rich and diverse professional life. So, embrace the benefits of early entrepreneurship and let it shape a promising future.

Steps to further develop your entrepreneurial skills

The entrepreneurial path is a never-ending journey, a winding road constantly enlightened by continuous learning and personal development. If you embraced the world of entrepreneurship at a young age, here are some crucial steps to continue honing and developing your skills:

1. Lifelong learning: Entrepreneurship is a constantly evolving playground. Continue to learn new trends, understand market developments and explore the latest technologies. Stay hungry for knowledge.

2. Continuing Education: Invest in your continuing education. Online courses, workshops, conferences and even academic programs can provide you with new perspectives and skills to fuel your entrepreneurial journey.

3. Active Networking: Cultivate your professional network. Attend events, engage in online forums, connect with other entrepreneurs. Networking offers opportunities, advice and a supportive community.

4. Mentoring: Always look for mentors who can guide you. Experienced entrepreneurs can offer valuable advice based on their own experiences. A mentor can also help expand your network and accelerate your professional growth.

5. Side projects: Don't rest on your laurels. Take on side projects to diversify your skills. Whether it's a new venture or an exciting project, it keeps you learning and growing.

6. Adaptability: Be ready to adapt. The entrepreneurial environment is dynamic, and the ability to adjust your strategy and evolve with circumstances is an invaluable skill.

7. Time Management: Effective time management is crucial. Balance your efforts between work, learning and rest. Good time management maximizes productivity and well-being.

8. Perseverance: Failure is an integral part of entrepreneurship. Cultivate perseverance and resilience. Every challenge is an opportunity to learn and grow.

9. Continuous Innovation: Innovation is the key to continued success. Always be on the lookout for new ideas, new approaches and new solutions.

10. Social Contribution: As an entrepreneur, look for ways to contribute socially. Whether it's through mentoring other young entrepreneurs, charitable initiatives or other forms of involvement, it enriches your entrepreneurial experience.

In conclusion, the entrepreneurial journey is an adventure that requires an ongoing commitment to learning and personal development. These steps can serve as a guide to propel you to new heights in your entrepreneurial career. So keep exploring, learning and growing - your entrepreneurial potential is limitless.

Towards New Horizons

Congratulations, young entrepreneur, on embarking on this exciting journey into the world of entrepreneurship. This book is just a stepping stone, an initial guide to arming yourself with the necessary skills and knowledge. The real learning is in the action, in the challenges you face and the successes you celebrate.

Never forget that every step you take now forms the path to your entrepreneurial future. The ups and downs are an integral part of this adventure, and every experience is an opportunity to learn and grow.

Remember, every successful entrepreneur started somewhere, often with a simple idea and a dose of audacity. Your dreams are the fuel of your journey, and your perseverance is the key that opens the doors to success.

So keep dreaming big, learning relentlessly and acting with determination. Your potential is unlimited, and every challenge is an opportunity in disguise. May this book be a constant source of inspiration on your road to new horizons. The world awaits you with its infinite possibilities. Thank you for your passion, courage and determination. May your future be as bright as your wildest dreams.

Here's to you, and to all the opportunities that await you,

Marcel Aoudi

Marcel Aoudi

tassguernine@gmail.com